LEICESTERSHIRE
MEMORIES

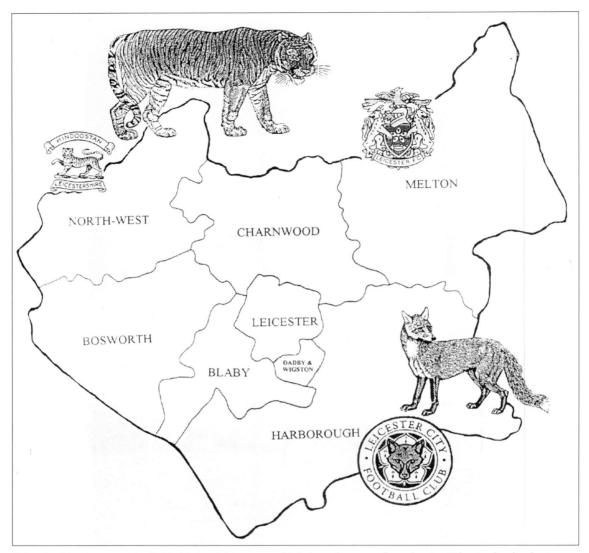

Leicestershire is a county divided into eight areas, which have been used as chapter titles in this book. Across the county the names of two animals appear again and again – the tiger and the fox. Various battalions of the Leicestershire Regiment spent long, arduous years in India, especially on the North-West Frontier, and were granted the emblem of a tiger as their cap badge. This animal was later adopted by the County Rugby Club, which still displays two tigers on its crest. During the First World War a company commander in the front line climbed over the parapet of his trench leading a charge of the 'Leicester' towards the enemy lines, kicking a rugby ball forward and shouting 'come on the tigers'. The 'tigers' fought in all theatres of war; during both world wars, and gained many battle honours. In peacetime the 'tigers' of the County Rugby Club now uphold the victory tradition, winning many honours.

Fox hunting and Leicestershire go together. Four famous hunts are centred on the county: the Quorn, the Belvoir, the Cottesmore and the Fernie. As a result of this activity the fox is incorporated in many emblems associated with the county. Leicester City Football Club's badge is especially well known and its fox denotes speed and cunning. 'The Foxes', a club with a long history, have achieved much in recent years. Based at Filbert Street in the city of Leicester, they are an inspiration to a wide range of people, young and old!

LEICESTERSHIRE
MEMORIES

TREVOR HICKMAN

SUTTON PUBLISHING

First published in the United Kingdom in 1999 by
Sutton Publishing Limited · Phoenix Mill
Thrupp · Stroud · Gloucestershire · GL5 2BU

British Library Cataloguing in Publication Data
A catalogue record for this book is available from the British Library

ISBN 0 7509 2287 7

Title page photograph: Burrough Hill, 1922.

By the same author:

Around Melton Mowbray in Old Photographs   *East of Leicester in Old Photographs*
Melton Mowbray in Old Photographs   *The Melton Mowbray Album*
The Vale of Belvoir in Old Photographs   *The History of the Melton Mowbray Pork Pie*
The History of Stilton Cheese   *Melton Mowbray to Oakham*
Around Rutland in Old Photographs

 TM ALAN SUTTON^{TM} and SUTTON^{TM} are the
trade marks of Sutton Publishing Limited

Typeset in 11/14pt Photina.
Typesetting and origination by
Sutton Publishing Limited
Printed in Great Britain by
Butler & Tanner, Frome, Somerset.

Contents

Heroes

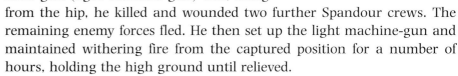

One of the author's lasting memories is of Dick Burton VC being introduced to the whole school at the Melton Mowbray Modern, in spring 1945. An old boy, he was given a standing ovation at morning assembly. As for all children of the 1930s, for the author war was very real: the 1914–18 conflict was very fresh in his parents' minds and his childhood was totally dominated by the Second World War. Heroes such as Dick Burton (below) and William 'Bill' Buckingham (right) were men who were looked up to by young impressionable schoolboys.

Dick Burton won his VC at the battle on Monte Ceco in Italy on 8 October 1944. A private in the Duke of Wellington (West Riding) Regiment, he had already showed outstanding courage in the North Africa campaigns. In the October offensive the Duke of Wellington platoon was instructed to take the 760 metres high Monte Ceco ridge, which was protected by German troops with four Spandour machine-guns. In the initial charge the platoon commander was wounded and many of Dick's comrades were killed. Dick continued the charge alone; killing the crew of three on the first Spandour, he then attacked the next two positions, his tommy-gun jammed, he retreated picked up a Bren gun (light machine-gun) and, firing

from the hip, he killed and wounded two further Spandour crews. The remaining enemy forces fled. He then set up the light machine-gun and maintained withering fire from the captured position for a number of hours, holding the high ground until relieved.

William Buckingham was awarded his VC for conspicuous bravery at the Battle of Neuve Chapelle on the Western Front on 10 and 12 March 1915. Bill was a private in the 2nd Battalion of the Leicestershire Regiment. Climbing out of the secure trench on the front line, he went to the aid of many of his wounded comrades dragging them back to safety under heavy enemy rifle and machine-gun fire. Not only did he rescue his own wounded comrades, it is on record that he gave assistance to a severely injured German. To quote Bill Buckingham: 'I came upon a badly wounded German soldier. One of his legs had been blown off. He was lying right in the fire zone. His piteous appeal for help – well, I rendered first aid as well as I could and just carried him to a place of safety.'

Introduction

When it was suggested that I should compile a photographic and illustrated record of Leicestershire I was extremely flattered but slightly overawed by the prospect. Having collected photographs, drawings, ephemera and books about the county of Leicestershire for over forty years I realised only too well what a challenge this would be; the title of the book was an incentive and a help – *Leicestershire Memories*. No one person can put together in one volume a complete record of such an interesting county. What can be done, and what I hope I have achieved, is the compilation of a book of personal memories.

The foundations upon which I have based this book are strong. Not only do I collect published works on the county but also for over twenty-five years I was involved with two publishing businesses that produced a number of excellent books concerning many aspects of the county's history – the Brewhouse Private Press and Sycamore Press Ltd. The Brewhouse Press began printing in 1962 and was a joint venture with my good friend Rigby Graham. The first book was released in 1964 and for twenty years we published a whole variety of works, all different but all with an art bias, and most were illustrated by Rigby in a variety of ways. Both of us are interested in the county of Leicestershire and this resulted in visits to unusual areas not considered to be on the 'tourist trail', such as deserted windmills, mine workings, airfields, derelict factories, railway tracks and long disused canals. Some most unusual books were published and today they have become collector's items. All Brewhouse Press books were issued as limited editions, some very small editions indeed, and only a few are specifically related to Leicestershire. However, my main interest in publishing and compiling books has been local history, especially illustrated local history. In 1977 I formed Sycamore Press Ltd with David Tew to publish books devoted to local history and especially Leicestershire local history. This publishing house operated for ten years, publishing more than twenty-five specialised books. Undoubtedly the most splendid and spectacular was Rigby Graham's *Leicestershire*, a large book in every sense, issued in a slip case, best described as a most unusual coffee-table book full of evocative and controversial line drawings and colour plates, all by Rigby.

Three books that contributed much to the published word on Leicestershire history were Jack Brownlow's book on Melton Mowbray, Peter Foss's *History of Market Bosworth* and John Barber's *History of Oakham School*. Through becoming involved with the authors of these works and others, and through taking many of the black and white photographs used in twenty-odd volumes, I travelled to most corners of the county, building up a photographic archive that I am now drawing on to compile this book. I have divided *Leicestershire Memories* into chapters based on the county's various boroughs and councils. The selection is mine and I apologise for not including a photograph of every village and hamlet – this was not possible. All the county's market towns are included and a few pages have been devoted to the city of Leicester. In recent years many publications have been issued in the British Isles that are totally concerned with publishing a photographic record of a given area. Leicestershire is no exception. The publishers of this book have released over twenty titles devoted to the county of Leicestershire of which most are photographic records of districts or areas on specific themes. What I have attempted to do in these pages is not duplicate too much of what has already been published by other authors. I have written and compiled books on the area around Melton Mowbray and they are listed on page 4; with the exception of *The History of Stilton Cheese* and *The History of the Melton Mowbray Pork Pie* they are photographic collections and, in a sense, complement this publication. I have not devoted many pages to Leicester itself and I recommend to the reader Sutton Publishing's other books on the city.

I would like to think that readers will consider this book worthy of joining the large list of titles about the county that have been printed over the centuries, starting with William Burton's *Leicestershire*, published in 1622. Of the histories published in earlier centuries, I consider John Throsby's *Memoirs of the Town and County of Leicester* (released in six small volumes, the first published in 1777) the most interesting. Throsby travelled around the Leicestershire collecting accounts of local history from a variety of sources and engravings of the drawings he made are scattered throughout the text in Throsby's small set of books. By modern standards the books are compiled in a most unusual way. What I enjoy most are the curious and apparently unrelated footnotes. Volume One closes with a paragraph that is totally unrelated to the foregoing text. At the time Throsby was writing he records the fact that it cost a farmer 4*s* a week to hire an ox or labouring horse, a pig was worth 1*s* and a fine fleeced sheep was worth 10*d*. Those six little books were not a complete record of Leicestershire – they were just a collection of interesting accounts. A few years later John Nichols published an eight-volume, large folio history of the county. This work contains a number of excellent engravings by a variety of artists and some have been included as illustrations in this book.

Writing the text that complements the pictures in this book has meant having to revisit many areas of the county, years after I first went to the locality. It has been a pleasure. Much has changed, especially when a village street is viewed 'thirty years on', but surprisingly some views have not altered at all and parts of Leicestershire are as rural as they have ever been. Unfortunately I cannot say that the urban areas remain the same. In my opinion modern planners have a lot to answer for, but, then, what would I have said if I had attempted to compile a book such as this when the Victorian planners were laying out the Great Central railway and demolishing most of the thatched buildings in the centre of Leicester? It's called progress, and I hope this collection is a record not only of what survives but also of what has changed in the name of progress. Perhaps, in years to come, some reader will get as much enjoyment out of this book as I do when I browse through John Throsby's little books, published over 200 years ago.

Trevor Hickman
October 1999

Charnwood

From the hill of Old John in Bradgate Park there are magnificent views of the woodlands of Charnwood, and villages and towns can be picked out on the horizon. Drive around the borough, and in the distance high on the skyline stands Old John. Photographed here in about 1910, the tower was built in 1786 by the Earl of Stamford on the site of a disused post-mill to commemorate an old retainer, John, who was killed at a bonfire party celebrating the coming of age of the Earl's grandson. John liked his ale, so this eye-catcher was built to look like a beer mug. In actual fact its purpose was to stand as a stone-built hunting tower so that the Earl's female guests could watch in comfort while their husbands hunted the deer in the park below.

WYMESWOLD

A drawing of the Main Street, Wymeswold in 1846 with the church of St Mary in the background. The Vicar at this time was the Revd Henry Alford MA, who was also a private school teacher. This is a typical scene of the nineteenth-century agricultural village that became a centre for fine Stilton cheese production. Four dairies were operating in the village in 1914.

The windmill, *c.* 1930. During the 1890s Joseph Hardy was the miller, and he was followed by James Pritchard in 1908. The mill ceased working during the First World War in 1916. It became derelict and was finally to be demolished in 1950. The four sails powered two pairs of stones with a flour dresser.

The main street, Wymeswold, seen from the tower of St Mary's church, 1903.

A similar view to the drawing illustrated above, 1904. The Vicar of St Mary's was now the Revd Robert Charles Green MA.

BARROW ON SOAR

Industry Square and the recently erected war memorial to the local lads who lost their lives in the First World War, 1925.

Tom Corbett's shop, 68 High Street, 1920s. Tom was also a hairdresser. As its name suggests Barrow is situated on the River Soar and is a haven for boat owners.

The Grammar School, 1904. It was founded by an endowment by the Revd Humphrey Perkins in 1717 and when this picture was taken the Headmaster was Frederick Ellison BA.

Barrow on Soar water-mill, c. 1910. In the Domesday survey in the eleventh century Barrow is listed as having three water-mills. The mill illustrated was powered by two large wheels that drove four pairs of stones for grinding corn. During its final years it ground gypsum; it was demolished in 1938.

LOUGHBOROUGH

A view of Loughborough drawn by John Throsby in 1790. The hills of Charnwood forest are in the background, the splendid church of All Saints is in the middle ground and the four-sail post-mill erected in the 1780s in the foreground. When the drawing was published as an engraving the town was little more than a village. Today all these fields have been covered by urban development.

A view of the bustling Market Place, 1906. To the right of the market are the premises of Constantine Dufner watchmaker at 33 Market Place. Next door (no. 35) is the Lord Nelson public house, whose landlord was James Gutteridge. The licence to hold a market in the town was granted in 1221. Market days are Thursdays and Saturdays.

Brush Electrical Engineering Co. Ltd, Falcon Engine and Car Works, Nottingham Road, 1906. 'The Brush' is an important part of Loughborough, and over the years has provided thousands of jobs for the local community.

The Quorn hunt holding its traditional Boxing Day meet in the Market Place, Loughborough, 1908. The Master of Foxhounds was Captain F. Forester. This once annual sporting spectacle has now been banned by the borough council.

Queens Park, laid out by the corporation to commemorate Queen Victoria's Diamond Jubilee in 1897, and the Carnegie Library, just before the First World War. The Carnegie Library was opened in 1905 by the Mayor Joseph Griggs. The bandstand on the left was erected at the expense of Councillor W.H. Wootton to mark the coronation of King Edward VII.

High Street, 1925. The Bull's Head Hotel sign is placed prominently across the highway; its landlord was James A. Hartopp. Signs such as this have their origins in gibbets erected outside stagecoach houses. Highway robbers were hung up on display as a deterrent to others. As many as six criminals could be suspended across the highway after a busy day at the assize courts.

In April 1999 Ladybird Books closed its doors. No more splendid children's books printed in Loughborough will travel to all countries of the world from this pioneering company. The company began when Wills & Hepworth, a local stationer and printer, decided to circumvent Second World War restrictions on paper usage by printing delightful little children's books on the stocks of white cartridge paper that they held; from these small beginnings a publishing empire developed. The success of the venture resulted in the business being sold by the original founder and the publishing house was subject to a number of take-over bids. But Ladybird did not want to stray from its original concept of designing and printing one book from one sheet of paper, and including a colourful hard-case binding.

The photograph at the top of the page shows ninety-year-old Mrs Anne Cashmore handing a collection of Ladybird books, presented in two specially bound book boxes covered in red and light blue morocco leather (bound by the author), to Princess Margaret for her two young children when she visited Loughborough on Friday 29 April 1966. In the centre of the group is the Mayor of Loughborough, Councillor G.H. Sharpe.

Below this are two title pages from one of the Ladybird book series *Talkabout Starting School*, one for sale in the English-speaking world and the other in the Arabic-speaking world. These show the breadth of publishing that this company achieved, bringing education to all quarters of the globe. It was a marvellous concept with authors, artists, designers, typesetters, printers, bookbinders, warehousing and marketing all under one roof. Unfortunately, current owner Penguin books does not believe that this method of production is viable for the twenty-first century.

QUORN

The centre of the village, 1910. To the left is the Royal Oak Inn and on the right is the White House Hotel, proprietor William F. Sheddon.

The Village Hall, 1904.

The Manor House Hotel, 1904, proprietor James A. Hartopp.

The existence of fox-hunting as we know it today is the result of Hugo Meynell's decision to form the Quorn Hunt. Born in 1727, Hugo inherited a vast fortune at a very early age and like all his contemporaries took to hunting deer on horseback, but because of land clearance this was a declining sport and fox hunting was on the increase. While still in his early twenties Hugo had realised, unlike his predecessors and fellow fox hunters, that chasing a fox with a pack of hounds willy-nilly across the countryside might be good entertainment but the real hunting, riding hard, jumping the high fences and deep ditches of the recently enclosed fields south of Nottingham through the Leicestershire Wolds provided the true excitement of the chase. He bred fast running hounds capable of keeping up with the fox.

The Quorn Hunt Kennels, near Quorn, c. 1910.

A Quorn hound begging for tit-bits from a kennel man at the hunt kennels, c. 1910.

A meet of the Quorn hounds at the village of Quorn during the 1910–11 season. The Master of Foxhounds was Captain F. Forester.

Quorn hounds being exercised in parkland near the village of Quorn by the huntsmen Tom Bishop and George Leaf, c. 1910.

ANSTEY

Church Bridge, a packhorse bridge off of the village green in Anstey, is the site of one of the first bridges ever to be built in this area of the East Midlands. Archaeological evidence points towards the present bridge being on the line of an ancient trading route from what is now Scandinavia to the west coast of Ireland. The 'Eldorado' route of the Bronze Age was used by the very first packhorse teams. Bronze Age tribes placed extremely high value on Irish gold, and a trading route across the North Sea to ports on the navigable rivers feeding into the Wash was established to bring the gold into northern Europe. The present granite bridge crosses the main arm of the Rothley Brook that rises in Charnwood Forest, a tributary of the Soar that runs through Thurcaston and Rothley. The restored fourteenth-century structure, built when Anstey was a hamlet in the parish of Thurcaston, is a five-arched bridge with four cut-waters facing the flow and the same number on the lee side. Each cut-water has a recess built above, for pedestrians.

King William's Bridge on the public footpath leading into Castle Hill public park. Constructed of granite, it straddles the northern arm of Anstey Brook that rises between Anstey and Cropston. Originally, the line of the present footpath was the road from Anstey to Bradgate Park, routed through Cropston and Hallgates. This road was an important highway in the seventeenth century, allowing the Earls of Stamford access to their extensive estates in the area. In the summer of 1696 King William III visited the Earl of Stamford at Bradgate Park. The King was conveyed through the Leicestershire countryside across the Earl's land. This packhorse bridge was widened to take the King's carriage. It is possible that the whole bridge was rebuilt and the recess constructed above the cut-water at this time to allow a faithful retainer or servant to conduct the King's horses over the arched roadway without incident. There seems little point in having a recess on such a short bridge.

THURCASTON

Sandham Bridge is certainly the least altered packhorse bridge in Leicestershire. It now carries the bridleway from the Anstey–Thurcaston road to Cropston, where it crosses the Rothley Brook. This unique bridge was almost certainly built in the fourteenth century by the Ferrers family, lords of the manor of Cropston and part of the parish of Thurcaston. Henry de Ferrers, Lord of the combined manor and Knight of Groby, died in 1387. The Ferrers family came to England with William the Conqueror in 1066 and were granted vast tracts of Leicestershire as reward for supporting the King in his campaign throughout the kingdom.

Bishop Latimer's house, *c.* 1790. The martyr Latimer was born in 1470. His father was a very successful local yeoman farmer employing twelve people, who was required to pay homage to the King, even raising a local force in support of King Henry VIII and travelling into Cornwall to help defeat the Cornish rebels headed by Lord Audley on 22 June 1497. Hugh would have been twenty-seven years old at this time, and managed his father's farm while he was away. He entered the church and was eventually ordained. Bishop Latimer was a supporter of the Protestant faith and one of Leicestershire's greatest sons. He was burnt at the stake on the instructions of Queen Mary I who attempted to return the country to Catholicism after the death of Edward VI. Latimer was burnt alive with Bishop Ridley on the north side of the city of Oxford in a ditch near Balliol College on 18 October 1555. He was chained to the stake, two bags of gunpowder were tied under his arms and they ignited when the flames touched them, tearing his body asunder, and ensuring that his earthly remains were quickly consumed by fire. Latimer's house was demolished in about 1900.

MOUNTSORREL

The main road through the village, *c.* 1915.

Mountsorrel Lock, near Jelly's Wharf, on the Leicester Navigation, *c.* 1920. The waterway was officially declared open on 24 October 1794.

Unloading wheat at Mountsorrel water-mill, 1912, the year it ceased operating. Powered by two 12½ feet diameter wheels that drove six pairs of stones, the mill was demolished in 1960.

The cupola erected by Sir John Danvers, Bt, in about 1800 on the site of the market cross that was removed on his instructions a few years earlier. In the thirteenth century King Henry III granted an order for a market to be held in this village square; the market was discontinued in 1850. This photograph was taken on Good Friday 14 April 1911. Behind the stone columns is the Co-operative Society Ltd, general stores.

REARSBY

A view of Rearsby Brook and the main road, *c.* 1916.

In the centre of the village near the church stands a delightful packhorse bridge. This is a perfect example of a bridge to carry pedestrians and horses crossing a stream alongside a ford. Both ford and bridge continue to serve the local community as they have done for hundreds of years. This stone bridge crosses the Rearsby Brook, a fast-flowing stream that rises in the parishes of Thorpe Stachville and Gaddesby, draining from a large watershed. When subjected to heavy rainfall the level of the brook rises rapidly, making the ford impassable. For many centuries the bridge was the only point at which the fast-flowing stream could be crossed, but there could have been more than one ford that was passable when the water was lower. It was built on the road from Gaddesby through Rearsby to Thrussington. The first bridge erected on the site of the present structure was a plank construction, possibly supported on stone and wooden pillars. In 1712 a charge was made of 10*d* against the parish by the constable in respect of repairing the bridge supports and replacing planks. In 1714 the parish paid for the present bridge to be built. The finance was raised by a levy on the local rates of 8*d* in the pound by the constable Robert Harrison: the total cost of building the bridge was £11 2*s* 2*d*. Over the sixth arch from the church end facing the flow the following is engraved on a key stone: R.H.1714. This bridge has been very well maintained. It consists of seven arches, although one arch on the south side has been virtually obliterated by the raising of the highway. There are six cut-waters facing the flow, none on the lee side. No pedestrian recesses exist because there was never any need for them on such a short bridge. It only ever carried local packhorses infrequently.

BIRSTALL

A romantic view of 'The Cottage' in the centre of Birstall, the home of the Revd James Went MA, 1916.

Lee Clayton and Andrew Tebbutt hand raising traditional Melton Mowbray pork pies in the bakehouse attached to Mark Patrick's butcher's shop on Sibson Road. Mark Patrick learned the skills necessary to produce excellent Melton Mowbray pork pies while working with Ralph Bramley in his shop at Queniborough when he left school. Today these excellent hand-raised pies are enjoyed by Mark's patrons, who recognise a quality product.

SYSTON

Broad Street, 1920. Syston is a village of straight streets possibly influenced by the Fosse Way, the Roman road that passes through the parish. For a more complete photographic record see pages 67 to 80 in *East of Leicester*, 1998.

Advertisement for W.H. Baldwin's board mill on the River Soar near Syston, 1892. This was a mill powered by a large water wheel driven by the fast flowing river. Water is an essential part of mill-board manufacture. The fibres are pulped, suspended in water and spread and strained on a wire mesh, prior to being rolled and consolidated into fibrous mass.

W. H. BALDWIN,
THE ORIGINAL HAND-MADE
LEATHER BOARD MANUFACTURER
Made from Scrap Leather, and are specially adapted for Stiffening for the Shoe Trade.

SOLE MANUFACTURER OF THE ORIGINAL HAND-MADE LEATHER BOARD,
The best Board in the Market for Blocking into proper shape.
SAMPLES AND PRICES ON APPLICATION.

SYSTON MILLS, NEAR LEICESTER.
TWENTY MINUTES' WALK FROM SYSTON STATION.

The Bowers family outside their home, The Fosse, Syston. During the 1890s and up to the end of 1900 Thomas Edward Bowers was the stationmaster at the Midland Railway station.

THRINGSTONE

Grace Dieu Brook, Thringstone, *c.* 1950. The stream was named after the Augustinian priory that stood near the village.

About the year 1239 a priory was built here for Augustinian nuns. This engraving depicts a nun in the kind of habit that would have been worn in the fifteenth century.

Ruins of the Augustinian priory still stand in the heathland off the Loughborough to Ashby-de-la-Zouch road, though they are in a parlous state. This engraving of Grace Dieu Priory was made in 1730 after a drawing by the artists and engravers Samuel and Nathaniel Buck. Henry VIII dissolved the priory in 1538. In 1539 the building was acquired by John Beaumont, who converted it into a private house in 1552. He fell out of favour, the house became deserted and was plundered for its stone.

ROTHLEY

The medieval half-timbered cottages off Town Green, Rothley, 1912.

Rothley Temple, 1905. This building gets its name from the Knights Templar who lived here. The late thirteenth-century chapel is one of the finest surviving religious buildings once occupied by this order in England. The hall is a mixture of Elizabethan and Victorian architecture. Today it is a fine country house hotel, Rothley Court. It has a splendid restaurant with thirty-four en-suite bedrooms divided between the main house and the converted stable block.

Fowke Street, *c.* 1910. To the right stands a thatched medieval half-timbered cottage. Note the steps and block used for mounting a horse.

Farnham's Bridge, 1934.

Farnham's Bridge, 1994.

John Ogilby, the seventeenth-century cartographer, showed a bridge of five arches. It is recorded in the minutes of the turnpike trustees as a packhorse bridge known as Farnham's Bridge, and was widened by this organisation in 1749. Prior to the widening of the structure, all horse-drawn vehicles used the ford across the upper reaches of the brook to the west, near the village of Rothley, pedestrians and packhorses using the narrow bridge. The name Farnham is attributed to the ancient Quorn family and it is possible that they built this packhorse bridge and financed its upkeep. Thomas Farnham owned extensive property nationwide and was honoured with the office of one of the Tellers of the Exchequer to the teenage King Edward VI in 1552. As a regular traveller he was so irritated by the need to ford the Rothley Brook, which repeatedly suffers from flash floods, that he commissioned the building of the packhorse bridge. Thomas Bown was commissioned by the turnpike trustees in 1798 to widen the bridge and construct a stout parapet on each side of the highway. Bown's builders virtually reconstructed the whole bridge in brick retaining part of the old packhorse bridge in the new. On completion, the four-arched bridge had a slate tablet positioned over the second arch from the south carrying the following: 27th June 1798. T.B.S. A new concrete bridge carrying the A6 was opened in 1991 on the Mountsorrel bypass, a few yards to the east of Farnham's Bridge and it is seen here on this aerial photograph, taken in autumn 1994. On close examination of the top right-hand photograph it is possible to see two arches of the early bridge incorporated into the present arches; possibly one was part of the original packhorse bridge. Evidence of stone and early brick are clearly seen when visiting the site.

WOODHOUSE EAVES

A general view of the village, the preserved windmill standing high on the skyline, *c.* 1905.

Woodhouse Windmill, *c.* 1905. In 1863 John Hives was miller and he ran the mill until 24 March 1895 when the whole structure was damaged in a severe gale. It was not considered a viable proposition to repair the mechanism, which included three pairs of stones. Because this post-mill stood in such a prominent position, it was decided to preserve the exterior and erect a set of sails. Continuous repairs took place over the years to keep the exterior in a sound condition, but all to no avail: in August 1945 it caught fire and was completely burnt down.

Main Street, 1907. The tower of the church of St Paul stands high in the background; it had been rebuilt in 1904. The Vicar in 1907 was the Revd A.J.W. Hiley MA.

ULVERSCROFT

Ulverscroft Priory drawn by John Throsby and engraved by J. Walker, 1790. This is the largest monastic ruin in the county of Leicestershire. Built on the instructions of Robert, Earl of Leicester, in 1134, it housed three hermits. In 1174 it was granted to the Augustinian order and became a priory. It was dissolved in 1539 on the instructions of Henry VIII and was purchased by the Earl of Rutland.

The ruins of Ulverscroft Priory, *c.* 1920. It is now part of a farm. In this photograph the guest hall is being used as a barn.

BRADGATE PARK

The ruins of the mansion house in Bradgate Park. The Marquis of Dorset began building a house on this site in 1490. After being passed between various owners it became unoccupied in 1719. This engraving was produced in 1793 by John Cary from a drawing by John Pridden.

An engraving of Lady Jane Grey at the age of sixteen. Lady Jane Grey was born at Bradgate House in October 1537 and developed into a clever studious child. Unfortunately, she was related to Henry VIII. Her cousin, Henry's only son, was a sickly child and was destined to be King Edward VI. He ascended the throne but at the age of fifteen he died. Edward VI had two half sisters, Mary and Elizabeth, but Henry VIII had disinherited them both. The most powerful nobleman in England was John Dudley, Duke of Northumberland. A favourite of Henry VIII, he realised that if either Mary or Elizabeth gained the throne he would lose power. He attempted to have Jane Grey's mother, the daughter of Henry VIII's sister, made queen but she refused to comply with the plans, preferring that her daughter should be crowned instead. Jane was forced to marry the Duke of Northumberland's son, Lord Guildford Dudley. On the death of Edward VI, Lady Jane Grey was proclaimed Queen by the Duke of Northumberland at Syon House, near Kew. She boarded a boat on the River Thames and proceeded to the Tower of London, which was to be her palace. However, the people objected and an army was raised in support of Mary. The Duke of Northumberland and Jane's parents saw that their cause was hopeless, and Jane abdicated after only nine days. Mary had the Duke of Northumberland beheaded. Jane and her husband were held as prisoners in the Tower. Unfortunately, Jane's father was subsequently involved in a plot to remove Mary and have Elizabeth crowned Queen. Mary had all the conspirators condemned to death and on 12 February 1554 Jane and her husband were beheaded on Tower Hill.

The ruins of Bradgate House, 1906.
Built by Thomas Grey, Marquis of
Dorset, between the years 1490 and
1505, largely of brick, it was the home
of Lady Jane Grey, the nine-day queen.
When she was executed the foresters
pollarded all the oaks in the park in
protest; today some of these oaks still
survive. The house and surrounding
land were enclosed in the seventeenth
century. William III stayed here in
1696. The Grey family abandoned the
house in the 1730s to live in their
property at Enville in Staffordshire.

The entrance to Bradgate Park, *c.* 1930.
In 1929 Bradgate Park was put up for
sale by the Grey family. It was
purchased by the Leicester
businessman Charles Bennion who
presented it to the city and county of
Leicester to be open space in
perpetuity. The park belongs to the
people, is administered by
Leicestershire County Council and is
open every day.

A picnic party at Old John, *c.* 1910.

GARENDON

Garendon Hall, a Palladian house built on the site of a Cistercian abbey, *c.* 1790. Dissolved as an abbey in 1536 by Henry VIII and bought by the Earl of Rutland, whose family sold it to Sir Ambrose Phillips in 1683, it was much altered in the 1860s by the architect Augustus Pugin and his son. This fine hall was totally demolished in 1964.

Stonebow Bridge, 1905. The granite structure was built in Pear Tree Wood on what is now the edge of Garendon Park. When viewed from a distance it looks like a medieval longbow as it spans the fast flowing Blackbrook close to the expanding town of Loughborough, which has absorbed the hamlet of Thorpe Acre that stood for centuries near this ancient stone bridge. The stream that the bridge crosses rises out of the rocks in Charnwood Forest and is fed by the Carr Brook where it joins the Blackbrook at Shepshed. A main feeder rises in Garendon and is controlled by a series of weirs that have enabled the ornamental lakes of today and the fishponds (stews) of yesteryear to become a feature of the parkland of Garendon.

This packhorse bridge stands on the route from Dishley Grange to Garendon Abbey. The abbey of the Blessed Virgin Mary was founded by Robert Bussu (Robert Crookback, Earl of Leicester) in 1133 for the Cistercian order. Even though it was only a small abbey (at the time of the Dissolution of the Monasteries in the sixteenth century only fourteen monks were in residence) Garendon controlled a number of granges – Dishley, 2 miles to the north-east, being one of them. This bridge was possibly first built in the late thirteenth century during the time of the Abbot Robert de Thorpe. As the abbey became more prosperous, more land was endowed to the holdings and demand for agricultural produce increased. Dishley became one of the main sources of supply. This grange generated large quantities of beef, mutton, venison, poultry and a whole range of cereal and root crops, reaching a peak of production in the sixteenth century, when horse-drawn carts replaced packhorses as a means of transporting goods from this very successful farm to the abbey. The packhorse bridge was widened at this time to take horse-drawn vehicles.

Dishley had become a centre for cereal production as early as 1252; horse-drawn vehicles were transporting grain to Garendon in 1534, two years prior to the dissolution of the abbey. Most of the estate was purchased by Ambrose Phillips and still remains in his family's hands.

Leicester Imperial Yeomanry at camp in
Garendon Park, 1904.

The Leicestershire Regiment at camp in
Garendon Park, 1909.

An eye-catcher in Garendon Park, the Temple of Venus, 1904.
It was designed by and built to the instructions of Ambrose
Phillips after he went on a Grand Tour of France and Italy in
1729. This structure was based on drawings he made of the
Temple of Vesta in Rome. A statue of Venus was erected inside
the monument, but it was destroyed in 1811.

BARKBY

Cows grazing in the park in front of Barkby Hall, the home of George William Pochin DL, JP, 1925.

Brookside, 1925. The Brookside public house stood on this lane and its landlord at this time was Robert Wyatt.

A Midland Railway 4–4–0 on the embankment, Barkby Lane, travelling from Nottingham to Leicester, April 1938.

NEWTOWN LINFORD

The Bradgate Hotel on the main road through Newtown Linford, 1904. The licensee was Harry Freeman Beck.

A medieval cruck-built house in Newtown Linford, photographed in August 1949 by Raymond Webster.

CÔTES

The thirteen-arched bridge at Côtes with Lower Côtes water-mill in the background, 1793.

Travellers from Leicester and Coventry were crossing the Soar at Côtes and Loughborough Meadows well before the twelfth century. There was a raised causeway with protective parapets, pedestrian recesses and arched connecting bridges over the many streams that made up the river at this point. A bridge of some description, possibly wood, crossed the river in 1086 and had been built by the Saxon landowners to serve the two water-mills that stood on this part of the Soar, later named Upper and Lower Côtes mills. Who built and maintained this long stone structure is not known, but possibly it was the first Saxon administration of any note. A substantial stone structure existed when King John rode along this packhorse route in 1209.

The hamlet of Côtes in the parish of Prestwold was granted by King Ethelred (reigned 978–1016) to the manor of Burton, which maintained a packhorse road to the main manor house in Staffordshire. After the Norman Conquest the hamlet remained under this administration for at least three centuries.

Thomas, Earl of Lancaster and Leicester, High Seneschal of England, massed his extensive army of 18,000 troops at Côtes Bridge in 1318 to intimidate King Edward II so that he could negotiate peaceable terms with the King, whose rule Lancaster did not accept. This hapless King was brutally murdered in Berkeley Castle, Gloucestershire, in 1327 having in the meantime lost the battle of Bannockburn to Robert Bruce.

Such an important crossing of a major Midlands river was bound to figure in the Civil War. On 20 March 1644 Sir Charles Lucas and Lord Loughborough were marching from Oxford to Newark with their troops. On arriving at Côtes Bridge they met the Parliamentarian forces under the command of Sir Edward Hartopp, who had marched from Leicester with Lord Grey's regiment to prevent the Royalists from crossing the Soar. A fierce battle ensued on and around the bridge when the roundheads, who were armed with three cannon, attacked the advancing cavaliers. Artilleryman Russell excelled himself with the accuracy of his shooting and the combined fire of the three cannon enabled the Parliamentarian troops to capture the bridge. This forced the Royalist forces to entrench and build a breastwork with five lines of trenches on the Loughborough side of the river. Here they remained all night. Hartopp eventually withdrew back to Leicester when he became aware that Prince Rupert was advancing on his position with 2,000 cavalrymen.

The present bridge carries the A60 Nottingham road and has been extensively changed over the last two centuries. The highway has been raised and the River Soar diverted into one main stream. It is built of red brick close to the line of the original causeway, but some evidence of an earlier stone structure can be seen on the lee side of the bridge under one of the seven arches when the river is low. Small modern cut-waters have been built to give an appearance of age and stonework has been retained under one of the arches. The river flows over a weir on the lee side, a few yards from the twentieth-century arches. The falling waters as they flow over these ancient stones deliver an excellent source of food for the shoals of large chub, which lie in the water with mouths agape catching the tasty morsels as they pass by in the rushing waters.

Melton

An aerial photograph of Melton Mowbray, possibly taken in 1925. Wilton Road had yet to be built, the east wing of Egerton Lodge was still standing and High Street ran round into Leicester Street. The formal gardens in front of Egerton Lodge are clearly shown as are the stables and horse training ring at the rear. The tennis courts on Leicester Road had yet to be built. In the background stand two gas-holders near to the Wyvern Knitting Wool Spinning Mill, then owned by T.W. Rust & Co.

WYMONDHAM

Above: The Duke of Rutland's Hounds, the Belvoir Hunt leaving the Berkeley Arms public house after meeting in the paddock at the rear at noon on 17 February 1999 to draw the plantation off Mount Pleasant Lane.

Right: Builder Tom Golling, who lived at Swiss Cottage on Spring Lane, feeding a runt of the litter that was eventually raised to become an enormous store pig, which was slaughtered in the autumn, thus providing hams, sides of bacon, and pork for pies and sausages. The photograph was possibly taken in 1935.

Pam Mason at 'The Spring', Spring Lane, 1955.

Wymondham Windmill, with horse-drawn steam-engine, bakehouse, pig sties and stables, *c*. 1905. The miller was Thomas Oldham.

A garden fête on the lawn in front of Sycamore House, the home of Richard Louis Fenwick, 1890s. In the centre of the group of ladies is Mrs Lee (dressed in black), the wife of the Revd William Hill Lee, the Vicar of Wymondham at that time.

A group of revellers at the Wymondham Badminton Club Ball held in the village hall, 1948. Back row, left to right: Vera Huckle, Walter Naylor, Brenda Talbot, Norman Wright, June Lewis, -?-. Front row: Beattie Cross, Mrs Yates, Nellie Huckle, Freda Stafford, Mrs Lewis.

A fête on the bowling green, Main Street, 1957. Background, left to right: Mrs Pye and the Revd Mr Pye (Vicar of Wymondham), Mrs R. Kirk and Mrs Keymer. Foreground: Andrew Goddard, Paul Tandy.

EDMONDTHORPE

Edmondthorpe Hall, the home of the Countess of Yarborough, with the lawn laid out for croquet, 1910.

The monument to Sir Roger Smith in the church of St Michael and All Angels. He died in 1655. Below Sir Roger lie the recumbent figures of his two wives. The lower one is his second wife Lady Ann, reputed to be a witch; at certain times of the year, it is said, the stain in the marble on her left hand bleeds. During her lifetime she was supposedly capable of turning into a white cat. The cook caught the white cat stealing in the kitchen and cut its left paw with a cleaver, hence the bleeding scar.

Hall Farm, off Woodwell Head Lane, Christmas 1904. It was the home of George Mariott for many years.

STAPLEFORD

An engraving by J. Walker of a drawing by John Throsby of Stapleford Hall, 1790. Note the recently built church of St Mary Magdalene to the left and the ruins of the Saxon church to the right.

A photograph taken in 1989 of the same view.

Lord Gretton standing outside the loco shed of Stapleford Miniature Railway, with one of his steam-engines on the turntable near the hall, 1970.

BUCKMINSTER

Buckminster Hall, the home of the Earl of Dysart JP, 1910.

Children standing on School Lane at the junction with Stainby Road, 1925. The iron railings on the corner were removed during the Second World War and melted down as scrap metal.

The main street, 1920. The Dysart Arms Hotel stands on the left in the middle distance and on the right is Thomson Skin's blacksmith shop.

SEWSTERN

The main street with the Blue Dog public house on the left, landlord Richard Edward Taylor, 1904.

The Red Lion public house, landlord Joshua Cole, 1916. For many years the county boundaries of Leicestershire and Lincolnshire passed through this hostelry. It was possible to purchase a pint in Leicestershire in the bar and walk into the lounge and drink it in Lincolnshire. This was especially interesting when the licensed opening times were half an hour longer in Lincolnshire, just after the Second World War.

Sewstern stands on the famous drove road the Sewstern Lane, which is now part of the Viking Way long-distance footpath. In the Middle Ages it was a very important highway and during the English Civil War in the seventeenth century it was a roadway that carried much ordnance and many troops, after the nearby Great North Road became impassable. The Red Lion was the venue for a most macabre incident. Nearby Belvoir Castle was a Royalist stronghold and to the south Burley-on-the-Hill was held by Parliamentarian forces. Many raiding parties scoured the countryside for provisions and on one such foray a skirmish took place at nearby Buckminster. Plukney, a captain of horse from Belvoir, was killed. The victorious roundheads under the leadership of Allen, a captain of horse from Burley, threw Plukney's body across his horse and proceeded to the Red Lion. The horse was tethered in the paddock while the roundheads refreshed themselves. Venturing out of the inn they encountered an avenging troop of horse from Belvoir and Allen was killed. The Royalists then proceeded to the Red Lion with the body of Allen thrown across his horse, which was tethered alongside Plukney's. According to a villager named Thorpe neither of the two was quite dead even though they had both been run through with swords, and they rolled their eyes at each other in agony until they passed away!

SALTBY

A Champion (Bellanca) Citabria two-seater tandem plane that was first flown in May 1964, at Saltby aerodrome in 1985. Laid out as a grass airfield, Saltby opened in August 1941 and became a satellite of Cottesmore, a few miles to the south. In the early years of the Second World War it was a major airfield equipped with Hampden, Anson and Wellington bombers and had the dubious distinction of being bombed by the Luftwaffe on three occasions. In February 1944 the Americans took over and it became USAAF Station 538.

Buckminster Flying Club glider, landing at Saltby, 1985.

The 1943 control tower, photographed in 1969.

Excavation of the Bronze Age barrow near Saltby aerodrome, 1978. This burial site was on land that was deforested in about 3900 BC. The burial site was constructed shortly after this date. The mound was supported by a low circular wall. The primary burial in the mound has been carbon dated to 1950 BC, which indicates the mound was in use for some 2,000 years!

BELVOIR

Belvoir Castle in 1790, an engraving by J. Walter of a drawing by John Throsby. It was rebuilt after the devastation of the Civil War but was more of a manor house on a hill than a castle. Fire partially destroyed the building in 1816.

Belvoir Castle, 1989. Rebuilt as a castle, it dominates the skyline when viewed from the Vale of Belvoir. It was completed in 1830 to a design by the Revd Sir John Thoroton – a marvellous mixture of towers and turrets, the fourth 'castle' on the site.

WALTHAM-ON-THE WOLDS

Church of St Mary Magdalene with its lychgate, 1925. The Vicar at this time was the Revd Bertell Hubert Smith MA, MC.

Waltham-on-the-Wolds Windmill, 1936. This tower-mill was built in 1868 and was worked by the Robinson family for many years. They sold it to Walter Owen in the 1920s, the sails were removed in 1941, and it was then driven by an oil-powered engine. It ground corn for animal feed until 1962, when it was sold for £750 and gutted for scrap iron. It was incorporated into a house in 1967. When working, the sail drove an iron upright shaft and brake wheel with a wooden rim; these powered three pairs of stones.

High Street from the church tower, 1925. On the left is the George and Dragon public house, where the licensee was John Rudkin Morris, who also ran the nearby Stilton cheese-producing dairy.

MELTON MOWBRAY

Melton Mowbray is world famous for its pork pies.
This is a prime example of a superb pork pie, baked
free standing and produced to the traditional recipe,
exclusive to this town and district, the centre for the
Melton Mowbray Pork Pie Association.

Lyndon Whittaker, Melton Mowbray pork pie *aficionado*,
holding a slice of the prize-winning pie presented by chef
Malcolm Gale at The Plough public house, Scalford, 1997.

Stephen Hallam of Dickinson & Morris, the famous
Melton Mowbray pork pie manufacturers, with the
international chef Gary Rhodes extolling the virtues of
this supreme pie, 1997.

45

South Parade, market day, 1904. On the right is the Holgate Boot Company and J.W. Warner's, printers, bookbinders, publishers, stationers, booksellers and library.

Selling sheep at Melton Mowbray cattle market off Scalford Road, *c.* 1920. The original sheep market in the medieval period was at the junction of Nottingham Street, High Street and South Parade. It took place around the sheep cross, later to be renamed the corn cross when the raising of sheep declined in the area as the enclosure awards took effect.

The new sheep pens in the rebuilt cattle market, 1999. This is now one of the leading outlets in England for the selling of sheep.

Market Place, *c.* 1940. It was dominated by the premises of bakery and restaurant owner Bill Warner, who specialised in producing traditional hand-raised Melton Mowbray pork pies.

The junction of Asfordby Road and Nottingham Road viewed from Park Road in about 1925 before Wilton Road was built to connect Leicester Road with Nottingham Road. The tree on the left is standing in the extensive grounds of Egerton Lodge, which were the eventual site of Barton bus garage, now demolished.

The Bricklayers Arms, Rutland Street, *c.* 1900. This public house was demolished just before the First World War and a more modern public house, also named the Bricklayers Arms, was built off Norman Way. Note the horse-drawn baker's van doing the rounds for Thomas Moore's bakehouse, which was situated at 1 Thorpe End.

One of the author's enduring memories is of being involved in publishing Jack Brownlow's splendid book, *Melton Mowbray Queen of the Shires*. Jack was a mine of information concerning the town of Melton Mowbray when it was the Mecca for all serious hunters of the fox. In the final stages of preparing Jack's manuscript for publication, much was revealed of the history of the town that has been most invaluable in assisting the author of this work in his researches. Today it is still a pleasure to browse through the pages of Jack's splendid history. In the photograph Jack is signing a copy of his book at the highly successful launch that was held at the Carnegie Museum on Tuesday 30 September 1980.

Four guests at the launch of the book *Melton Mowbray Queen of the Shires*. Left to right: Moira Ecob, Pam Hickman, Ian Hickman, Mary Jones.

TUMBLEDOWN FARM

Crosher's Lodge, off Spinney Road, Melton
Mowbray, 1980s.

Tumbledown Farm, late 1990s. Formerly Crosher's
Lodge, it opened to the public in 1996 as a working
farm keeping sheep, cattle, pigs, goats and poultry,
growing corn and maintaining hay meadows.
Conservation is a major theme and wild flowers are
encouraged in the meadows and hedgerows. Some
of the hedges are 800 years old. Children's parties
are welcomed and there is a challenging adventure
playground as well as supervised hands-on
experiences.

One of the occupants of the farm keeps a wary eye on the
photographer.

Mallard have flown in to visit some of the residents and
are also looking for food in the straw bedding.

LONG CLAWSON

The name of the village of Long Clawson is synonymous with excellent Stilton cheese manufacture. In this photograph Gary Cook and Phil Earl stir the milk and cut the curds in the vats, one of the first processes in cheese manufacture.

Tracey Mooney and Denise Wheat are preparing Stilton cheese so that a sound, thin crust will form while the cheese is maturing.

Karlis Doughty uses a sampling iron to take pieces from ten-week-old Stilton cheese to assess its quality.

RAGDALE

Ragdale Hall, the 'New Hall' built in 1785 when the Old Hall was converted into a farmhouse. The latter was demolished in 1958. In this photograph the castellated brick fantasy built in 1900 is covered in Virginia creeper. For many years this was the county seat of the Earl Ferrers.

Ragdale Hall is now a health hydro. In this photograph a guest is being welcomed in the reception area.

Among the many experiences on offer at Ragdale Hall is the water complex, incorporating two swimming pools. There is a 25 metre lane pool for the keen swimmer along with cascade and massage jets, two saunas, steam rooms, plunge pool and tropical bath. Part of the Ragdale experience is the enjoyment of good healthy food served in a fine restaurant by charming staff.

BOTTESFORD

Left: Market Street, featuring the market cross with the church of St Mary the Virgin standing high in the background, 1905. The Vicar at the time was the Revd Canon William Vincent-Jackson. *Above*: Tombs of the Dukes of Rutland in the church of St Mary the Virgin, 1920. One of them is the splendid monument to the 6th Duke of Rutland who died in 1632, his two wives and children. It bears an inscription, which runs: 'in 1608 [the Earl] married Lady Cecilia Hungerford, by whom he had two sons, both which died in infancy by wicked practice and sorcery'. It is the only inscription of its kind in England.

Bill Denning leaving Fleming's Bridge, 1993. The bridge is built across the River Devon on the south side of the church of St Mary the Virgin. The Devon, a fast-flowing stream that rises near Eaton and Croxton Kerriel, is a tributary of the River Trent. As it runs through the village of Bottesford it forms a loop around the church and until the seventeenth century this part of the village could be cut off for some days when the winter rains made the two fords impassable. In the winter of 1606 the Rector of Bottesford, Dr Samuel Fleming (Rector, 1581–1620), was returning from a visit to Leicester on horseback and attempted to cross the Devon at the south ford, when the river was swollen with flood water. The force of the torrent unseated him and he nearly drowned. He vowed that this would never happen again and at his own expense he had the small stone two-arched bridge constructed for pedestrians, horse-riders and packhorse teams. He purchased land at Frisby-on-the-Wreake to provide income for the upkeep of the bridge after his death.

While Fleming was Rector of Bottesford church, the infamous witches of Belvoir were operating in the Vale of Belvoir. Did Joan Flower and Anne Baker, along with Joan Willimott and Helen Green, cross this bridge to perform some evil practice in the churchyard in the early 1600s? Joan cheated death at the hands of the hangman when she dropped dead in the dock at her trial. The other three were all hanged at Lincoln gaol on 11 March 1619.

THORPE SATCHVILLE

The main street, *c.* 1915.

The Pinfold, the home of Captain Alfred Lowenstein, 1927. Captain Lowenstein lived at The Pinfold for a number of years during the 1920s. A very wealthy Belgium financier, he maintained a string of horses in the stables, supported the three local hunts and was a friend of the Prince of Wales, appearing as a guest at the Prince's many parties at Craven Lodge in nearby Melton Mowbray. Captain Lowenstein died in mysterious circumstances as a result of falling (or being pushed) from an aeroplane.

LEESTHORPE

Leesthorpe Hall, 1792, an engraving by John Walker of a drawing by John Throsby. At this time it was the home of John Suffield Brown, a local businessman who had interests in many local companies. It is possible that his family built the hall.

Leesthorpe Hall, 1989. The building's appearance is not unlike that of a French château. The lake that was made by damming a small stream is still there though the stone gothic 'eye-catcher' in the illustration at the top of the page has long since been removed.

ASFORDBY

Above: On the minor road from Kirby Bellars to Asfordby stands a narrow bridge that spans the River Wreake. Vehicles travelling over the bridge are controlled by a set of traffic lights. Incorporated into the present structure are the remains of the original medieval packhorse bridge that served this highway. Three arches remain, but there must have been more. Four cut-waters of varying ages face the flowing waters of the Wreake and on the lee side the remains of an early structure can be seen, retained under the bridge in the extension to the arches. The end of a curved cut-water is clearly visible some feet under the bridge. Originally built of hard local stone, it is now a hotchpotch of stone and twentieth-century brick. With the canalisation of the Wreake in 1797 the bridge was altered considerably and was maintained by the canal and highway authorities without any consideration for its historic past. It has suffered badly through lack of interest, as is evident in this photograph taken in 1993. *Left*: The church of All Saints, 1904. The Vicar at the time was the Revd Thomas Beaumont Burnaby MA. In the foreground stands the ancient market cross.

Blast furnaces at Asfordby Hill, *c*. 1925. The foundations for the first blast furnace were laid down in 1878 as a result of the discovery in 1874 of large quantities of iron ore in the neighbouring villages of Holwell and Ab Kettleby by Richard Dalgleish. He named the works Holwell Iron Company after the village where he first mined ironstone.

BROOKSBY

The church of St Michael at Brooksby Hall, drawn by J. Pridden and engraved by J. Cary, 9 July 1793. The hall has had some interesting owners over the centuries, commencing with the Villiers family, who came to England with William the Conqueror, laying out the Brooksby estates in about 1230. The family held the estate until 1711 when William, the last Villiers, died without heirs. In 1830 Lord James Bruchnell came to live in the hall and on the death of his father he became the 7th Earl of Cardigan. Extremely wealthy, he purchased a commission and was created a major-general in 1854. He achieved immortality by leading 'from the front' in the famous charge of the Light Brigade at Balaclava in the Crimean War in 1854. In all 673 mounted men charged the massed Russian guns; twenty minutes later 247 lay dead and 500 horses had been slain. The guns were over-run but the Light Brigade ceased to exist as a fighting unit. In 1906 the Beattys arrived at Brooksby. David Beatty had married a very wealthy lady Mrs Ethel Tree in 1901. Quickly gaining promotion, David Beatty attained the rank of Rear-Admiral at the age of thirty-nine in 1910. On 31 May 1916 he was the Vice-Admiral in charge of the British Fleet at the Battle of Jutland. He was made the Admiral of the Fleet on 3 April 1919. On his death in 1936 the estate passed to his son who sold it to the Leicestershire and Rutland County Councils in 1945.

In 1945 Brooksby Hall was in use as a training centre for servicemen returning to civilian life. In 1950 more land was purchased and the development of the famous agricultural college began. In this photograph students are handling ewes and lambs.

Training is extensive in all aspects of farmland management, including the construction of dry stone walls.

In this photograph students are being instructed in fish farming techniques, not only in trout farming but also the skills required to run public aquariums and zoos.

In addition to the educational facilities on offer at Brooksby College, another facility has been developed at the hall – a superb restaurant, with conference and banqueting facilities which are of a very high order.

As part of Brooksby Hall's promotion strategy the conference centre and restaurant was used in a Stilton cheese event on 23 December 1998 organised by the *Leicester Mercury*, which published a critical survey of all Stilton cheeses produced by the seven manufacturers. Featured in this photograph are Stilton rings from the seven dairies, and left to right are the panel of judges: Sharon Grech, lecturer from Southfields College and School of Catering; Pam Hickman, housewife; Trevor Hickman, author of *The History of Stilton Cheese*; Andrea Smith, Consumer Affairs Analyst for the *Leicester Mercury*; Edwina Baker-Courtenay, Hotel Services Manager, Brooksby College; Kevin Stanley, Head Chef, Brooksby College Restaurant.

BURROUGH-ON-THE-HILL

The main street looking west, with the entrance to Burrough House in the background, 1910. The village is situated approximately half a mile from the Iron Age fortress that dominates the landscape in this area of Leicestershire (see title page).

Burrough Court, 1910. The building burnt down during the Second World War. It was at this house that the Prince of Wales, eventually King Edward VIII, met the American divorcee Mrs Wallis Simpson, who was a guest of the then owner of Burrough Court, Viscount Furness. The Prince of Wales gave up his girlfriend of sixteen years, Winifred Dudley Ward (a married woman), with whom he rode to hounds with the Melton Mowbray hunts and the South Nottinghamshire, for Wallis.

KIRBY BELLARS

The Quorn hounds leading off at the Old Manor House, 1904. The Master of the Foxhounds was Captain J. Burns Hartopp, and the Huntsmen were Tom Firr, Walter Keyte and Tom Bishop.

A meet of the Quorn Hunt at Kirby Gate, 10 November 1919. Joint Masters of Foxhounds at this time were W.E. Paget and Major A.E. Burnaby. The Huntsmen were Walter Wilson and George Barker.

The Hunting Lodge, Kirby Cottage, the residence of Major Wilfrid Ricardo, 1904.

SAXELBY

Thatched cottages, *c.* 1920. They were pulled down before the Second World War to make way for more modern houses!

Group of Heifers Fed on White's Maize Germ Cake.
Owner:—Mr. HENRY MORRIS, SAXELBYE, MELTON MOWBRAY.

A group of Henry Morris's heifers prior to calving. This photograph appeared on an advertisement for cattle food. Eventually, after producing calves, the fifteen cows would produce about 50 gallons of milk per day, which was converted into three standard-sized Stilton cheeses in Henry's dairy in the centre of the village.

A meet of the Quorn Hunt at Saxelby Park, 30 March 1908. The Master of the Foxhounds was Captain F. Forester and the Huntsmen were Tom Bishop and George Leaf.

Harborough

Quenby Hall, a magnificent Jacobean house built of brick on the instructions of George Ashby between the years 1615 and 1620. This photograph, taken in March 1989, is of the view that all visitors to the hall get when they approach the house through its surrounding parkland. It is considered to be one of the finest stately homes of its type in England.

TILTON-ON-THE-HILL

By driving and walking haphazardly through the countryside of Leicestershire with the artist Rigby Graham over a thirty-year period the author came to know and love this county. Lasting memories are of Rigby drawing and painting evocative views, and many of the illustrations and paintings were published in books. This illustration was drawn on site in 1981 in the railway cutting adjacent to the derelict Tilton-on-the-Hill station at Halstead.

HALLATON

The unusual conical market cross surrounded with thatched cottages, *c.* 1910. Today the war memorial stands nearby.

Hallaton Rectory, the residence of the Revd William Chetwynd Stapylton MA, 1904.

High Street, *c.* 1910. The villages of Hallaton and nearby Medbourne have gained their place in English folklore as the venue for the annual Easter Monday bottle kicking and hare pie scramble.

MEDBOURNE

Church of St Giles, 1904. The Vicar was the Revd Charles Fryer Eastburn MA.

Medbourne tower-mill, c. 1900. It was demolished in 1902, and probably the last miller to grind corn was John Kirby.

This picturesque packhorse bridge straddles the Medbourne Brook near the church in a village steeped in history. The brook rises in Cranoe, Tugby, Hallaton and Horninghold; it feeds into the River Welland just south of the village. Medbourne parish is on the line of a Bronze Age road and late Celtic harness have been excavated at a site near the village. Extensive Roman remains have also been uncovered, including a large villa, which was excavated in the late eighteenth century. It is presumed that the present village was built on the site of a Roman army encampment. The Saxons occupied the site; their pottery and bronze artefacts have been found in this area over a number of years. Because of the nature and lie of the land it is hardly likely that a bridge was built over the brook that passes through the village by these early settlers because it was easily fordable for most of the year. The brook forms a curve around the western perimeter of the churchyard. This is part of the moat that encircled the church, almost certainly constructed during the reign of Stephen (1135–54), an age of anarchy. The church would have been a haven from the marauding, lawless bands of foreign mercenaries in the pay of the local barons. A bridge to the church would have been needed possibly across the west side over the Medbourne Brook but it would have been a drawbridge, not a permanent structure. After Stephen's death a new age began and ecclesiastical control was extended. In 1262 the manor of Medbourne was granted by Henry III to William Chaudeler, passing into the hands of John de Kirby, who at his death in 1290 was Bishop of Ely. It is presumed that the present bridge was constructed during this period.

MARKET HARBOROUGH

Market day, 1940s.

High Street, 1934. The Three Swans, formerly The Swan, first recorded as a hostelry in the town in 1517, is on the right. Standing high in the background is the imposing steeple of St Dionysius', the parish church.

High Street, 1904. The Three Swans Hotel is on the left: the proprietor at this time was R. Marriott. On the right stands Herrap Wood's music store at no. 62. He was a professor of music and organist at the parish church.

High Street with the Angel Hotel on the right, manageress Mrs Mary Wootton, 1905. A feature of the building at this time was the wooden Tuscan porch.

St Mary's Road, 1905.

Above: The 1614-built grammar school, Smith's Charity School, 1930. The unusual building was constructed on ten timber arches, which supported the school room. Above this is a loft that was for the schoolmaster's use. *Right:* Market Harborough post-mill in 1895, the year that it was demolished to make way for Symington's corset factory. Built in about 1800, it was run by the Smith family throughout its existence.

The sheep market in the town square, 1903, the year that it was closed.

The ancient bridge across the River Welland, 1905.

Foster & Hill's boathouses on the Grand Union Canal, Market Harborough, 1905.

FOXTON

Church of St Andrew, when the Vicar was the Revd William Scott MA, 1914. Next door is the Black Horse Inn, run by the Lichfield Brewery Co. and selling its fine ale and stout. The landlord was Harry W. Hemmings.

A general view of the village in the 1920s.

Children walking along the tow-path of the Grand Union Canal before the First World War.

Foxton inclined steam-powered boat lift that
operated from 1900 to 1911 – a good idea
that proved too expensive to operate.

A view of the boat lift from the basin on the
canal, c. 1905. Plans exist to restore and
rebuild this unique lift.

Foxton Locks, 1984. Completed in 1812 they
provide a spectacular rise of 75 feet and
cause considerable hold-up for barges using
the canal. To obviate this the boat lift was
installed.

KIBWORTH HARCOURT AND KIBWORTH BEAUCHAMP

The Kibworths were two separate villages when this delightful photograph was taken in Kibworth Harcourt off the Leicester to Market Harborough road before the First World War. Today a visitor to the area will find it very difficult to separate the two villages.

Kibworth Harcourt mill, 1924. This post-mill still stands near the village. Extensively repaired in 1936, it is still a complete windmill. It is the only surviving post-mill in Leicestershire and was possibly built in 1609.

Station Road, Kibworth Beauchamp, 1941. The photographer stood near the entrance to the railway station, which was opened on 8 May 1857 and closed on 1 January 1968. On the right is the public house, the Railway Arms – licensee Louis Joseph Wyatt.

GREAT GLENN

A girl feeding ducks from the bridge over the brook, 1905. This pleasant rural scene often changed after heavy rain when this stream became a raging torrent.

The mill house, 1905. A water-mill was listed at Great Glenn in the eleventh-century Domesday survey. The water-mill at this site ceased operating in 1885 and it was converted into the house shown in this photograph.

A delightful family scene with a child on a pony in Orchard Street, 1906.

BILLESDON

This is the site of the weekly Friday market granted to Billesdon in 1618, which was held around the market cross in front of the Old Greyhound Inn. The photograph was taken in 1905 when William John Neville Knight was the landlord and also the local chemist.

Long Lane, 1905.

Leicester Road, 1905.

Billesdon Coplow, 1904. This was the home of the Hon. Mrs E.A. Pelham. The house was built in the 1780s and this site was chosen because it is one of the most prominent features in Leicestershire – a wooded hill that stands 700 feet above sea level. The first point-to-point here with more than two runners took place in 1792 and the course was from Barkby Holt to Billesdon Coplow and back, a distance of 8 miles; the winner was Charles Meynell.

Billesdon & District Football Club, 1907/8. Back row, left to right: W. Stawson (Vice-President), W.J. Atcheson, T. Barnes, H. Wadkin, T. Vickers, H. Bent (Trainer). Middle row: J. Vickers, J. Cart, C.W. Stockford (Captain), J.E. Bent, A. Crane (Vice-Captain). Front row: A. Jassel, Alf Crane.

HUNGARTON

Above: Baptismal font with its unusual carved base, possibly of Saxon origin.

Left: The church of St John the Baptist, 1983.

Near the church stands a gravestone dedicated to Jonathan Godard, who passed away on 22 March 1763 aged sixty-nine. The engraving is by E.P. of Barkby who had a dry sense of humour: 'Reader stand still and shed a tear/Upon the dust that lieth here,/And as you view this state of mine,/Think of the glass that runs for thine.'

NOSELEY

Noseley Hall, 1791. It was built by the Hazlerigg family in the 1720s and this view is an engraving by J. Walker of a drawing by John Throsby. The church of St Mary stands to the left of the hall.

The lake at Noseley Hall with boathouse, 1905. The hall was the home of Sir Arthur Grey Hazlerigg Bt, JP at this time.

Noseley Hall in 1989, with the church of St Mary, now minus its tower, which was removed in 1793.

STOUGHTON

A general view of the village of Stoughton before the First World War.

The church of St Mary in 1916, when the Vicar was the Revd William Seaver who lived at nearby Thurnby.

This was a standard wartime airfield, built with three concrete runways with an encircling perimeter track, which still exists in part on the surrounding agricultural land. Situated near the village of Stoughton, it opened on 15 October 1943. The RAF withdrew from the airfield on 31 December 1947. It has since been developed as a civilian airfield and the Leicestershire Aero Club has repaired and now maintains much of the wartime site. Used extensively in the 1990s, the control tower adjacent to the wartime runway has been renovated. Standing on the grass is a Cessna 172, R.G. Cutlass.

FLECKNEY

High Street, 1925. On the right is the post office run by Percy Henry Preston.

A horse and cart loaded with milk churns on Mawby's Lane, 1925.

Kilby Road, 1940s.

Fleckney Guild football club, 1920/1. Percy 'Shaver' Badcock is in the centre of the front row, holding the ball.

Children playing on Gladstone Street, viewed from Saddington Road, before the First World War.

Watercolour of a greater spotted woodpecker by Jack Badcock of Fleckney, reproduced on the jacket of Jack's book *In the Countryside of South Leicestershire* (1972). The author has fond memories of discussing the countryside with Jack and had the pleasure of advising him on the publication of two of his books. In 1954 Jack began writing a weekly column for the *Leicester Mercury*, illustrated with his delightful line drawings, and he continued to do so for over eighteen years. In 1973 a collection of his writings was published under the title *A Countryman's Calendar*. Simon Garner, Editor of the *Leicester Mercury*, likened him to a modern-day Richard Jefferies, 'a masterly portrayer of the ever changing scenes of nature'.

HUSBANDS BOSWORTH

Right: High Street, 1904. The steeple of the church of All Saints is in the centre background. The Vicar was the Revd Maurice Lamb MA.

Husbands Bosworth School. 1925. The Headmaster was Ernest Drewitt.

Church Lane, 1940s.

STANFORD HALL

Stanford Hall in 1791, an engraving by J. Walker of a drawing by John Throsby. The building of this house began in 1697 under the directions of Sir Roger Cave. It is considered to be the finest house of this date in Leicestershire.

The lake and hall, 1989. Compare the photograph with the engraving above. Little has changed in almost 200 years! This hall is open to the public and is worth visiting. The village of Stanford is actually in Northamptonshire, across the River Avon. Its church has a memorial to an aviator who fitted an engine to a glider, but was killed in a crash landing in 1899.

MISTERTON

Misterton Hall in 1792, an engraving by J. Walker from a drawing by John Throsby. The church of St Leonard is to the right.

The hall and church, 1989. Changes have taken place since John Throsby produced the illustration above. In 1800 the hall was faced with brick, producing a Jacobean look. In the middle of the nineteenth century the gardens were terraced down to the lake. There was once a considerable village in this area but it was subject to a clearance programme in the fifteenth century, which converted the fields to pasture for sheep grazing. Now Misterton is little more than a hamlet with a hall and church.

LUTTERWORTH

This is a very informative photograph of Church Street, August 1904. A horse-drawn water carrier and pump is providing water to the occupants in the street; note the galvanised buckets. The water was supplied by the Lutterworth Freehold Land and Buildings Society. In the centre stands the church of St Mary the Virgin – the Vicar was the Revd Canon Frederick Cecil Anderson MA. On the right is Samuel Poole's bakery and grocer's shop, standing next to the Coach and Horses public house, where the landlord was William Holyoak.

Station Road, 1904. The ivy-covered house on the left was the home of the Revd Thomas Champness, a Wesleyan minister. The railway station was at Rye Hill on the Great Central line – and the Stationmaster was W. Barlow. It opened on 15 March 1899 and closed on 5 May 1969.

Bitteswell Road, 1920s.

Left: Bridge over the River Swift, which feeds into the River Avon, *c.* 1920.

Right: Spital Mill, 1892. The water-mill was built on the River Swift off the Rugby Road and ceased operating in the 1890s when the construction of the Great Central Railway cut off the water supply.

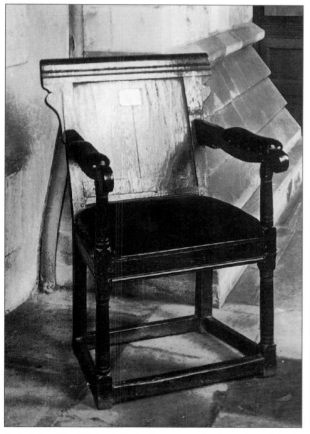

Left: John Wycliffe's chair in Lutterworth church, *c.* 1905. *Right*: The Wycliffe memorial in Lutterworth church, *c.* 1905. John Wycliffe (*c.* 1320–84) was an English reformer and international scholar. Elected master of Balliol College, Oxford, he was a leading figure in fourteenth-century political and ecclesiastical debates. On 28 December 1384 he had a fatal stroke and died on New Year's Eve while at Lutterworth where he was buried. By decree of the Council of Constance on 4 May 1415 his remains were ordered to be exhumed and burnt. This was carried out on the orders of Pope Martin V in 1428.

BROUGHTON ASTLEY

St Mary's church, with the fast-running stream and its stone bridge leading to the stile into the churchyard. The illustration by John Pridden dates from 22 June 1791.

Mill Lane, *c.* 1910. Note the splendid white-washed, half-timbered thatched house in the background.

The tributary of the River Soar with brick footbridge, *c.* 1905.

CLAYBROOKE MAGNA

The Atherstone Hunt outside the Bull's Head. The landlord at this time was George Brown, 1904.

Inside Claybrooke mill, *c.* 1970. This photograph shows the main shaft, bevel-geared crown wheel and grinding tun. The mill dates from the late seventeenth century and ceased operating in 1953. It was powered by a pitch-back, over-shot wooden wheel.

High Cross, *c.* 1930. The monument was erected in 1712. The Fosse Way and Watling Street, the famous Roman roads, cross at the edge of Claybrooke parish, which is often referred to as the centre of England. It is the site of the Roman settlement called Venonae.

WISTOW

Wistow Hall, 1790, an engraving by J. Walker of a drawing by John Throsby. The Jacobean house was much altered in 1810. It was the residence of the Halford family for many years and in 1645 Sir Richard Halford provided shelter for King Charles I and Prince Rupert after their crushing defeat by Cromwell's army at the Battle of Naseby. Changing horses, the King left behind his ornate saddlery, which was to be collected at a later date. He never returned and it has remained at the hall ever since.

Wistow Hall, 1989. The occupier of the hall from the 1790s until 1840 was Sir Henry Halford, physician to the Prince Regent, who gave him two emus that had been sent from Australia. These were allowed to roam throughout the park and became vicious pets, attacking everyone in sight. Lord Cottesloe occupied the house in the 1890s. He carried out many experiments on his private range in the interests of improving the rifle used by the British Army, and contributed to the accuracy of the weapon used by troops in the South African

Oadby & Wigston

A commemorative emblem published in 1928 showing some of the battle honours of the 17th Regiment of Foot, The Leicestershire Regiment. Many generations of young men were called to the colours from the towns and villages of Leicestershire and served in this famous regiment that had its headquarters at Wigston. Indeed, the author of this book walked through the imposing gates to the barracks on a bright September morning in 1952. The regiment was formed in 1688 under the command of Colonel Solomon Richard on the instructions of King James II, who was preparing the defence of the realm against an invasion from Holland. In 1751 it became the 17th of Foot. Over the centuries the regiment fought on every continent. At the turn of the nineteenth century the regiment began its long service in India taking part in gruelling campaigns on the North-West Frontier and in Afghanistan. On 25 June 1825 His Majesty King George IV announced that the regiment could bear 'on its colours and appointments the figure of the Royal Tiger with the words Hindoostan inscribed as a lasting testimony of the exemplary conduct of the corps during the period of its service in India from 1804 to 1823'.

Crow water-mill, *c.* 1925. There were two mills near each other on the Countesthorpe road south of Wigston – a post-mill and a water-mill. The water-mill ceased working in about 1900 when the miller was William Vice.

South Wigston railway station, *c.* 1910. It opened on 30 June 1840 and closed on 1 January 1962. The site has been developed and is now a health centre.

Station Road, Wigston Magna, *c.* 1905.

Bull Head Street, Wigston, *c.* 1925. The British School, a fee-paying school, is the tall building on the right.

Long Street and Leicester Road, 1916. On the left is Alfred King's chemist's shop at no. 50 Long Street, next door to William J. Cox, fruiterer, at 2 Leicester Road.

Aylestone Lane, Wigston, *c.* 1910.

The Cottage Homes, Oadby,
c. 1910. The cottages were
erected by the Worshipful
Company of Framework
Knitters in 1908.

Stoughton Drive, Oadby, *c.* 1910.

Leicester Road, Oadby, 1941.
The steeple of the church of St
Peter stands high in the centre
of the picture; its Vicar was
the Revd Bernard Ralph
Cooper BA. The antique shop
of Thomas E. Law is on the
right a few doors up from
Harold Moore's butcher's shop.

Stoughton Road, Oadby, 1930s.

Oadby Hill, 1920s.

Oadby Hill, 1940s.

This photograph of the entrance to Glen Parva Barracks, the headquarters of the Leicestershire Regiment, was taken in the 1920s. Reproduced as a postcard, it was sent to 4854066 Bandsman Tom Bradshaw of the 1st Battalion The Leicestershire Regiment, stationed at Purandhar, India, and arrived on 4 May 1929.

Emblem of the Royal Leicestershire Regiment. In 1946 King George VI ordained that the Leicestershire Regiment should become the Royal Leicestershire Regiment in recognition of its outstanding achievements during the Second World War. It is not possible to list here all the battle honours that this famous regiment received. However, it must be noted that it fought with General Wolfe in Canada, was given the tiger as a badge for service in India and saw action in the defence of Ladysmith in the Boer War. There was hardly a First World War battle that the 'Tigers' did not take part in. The author's uncle, Sidney Hickman, joined the 'Leicesters' and was killed at the second Battle of Arras. The regiment fought in every theatre of war between 1939 and 1945 and excelled itself in Korea in the 1950s.

Leicester

In this photograph, taken by Walter Coxhead in 1958, we can see the clock tower and Charles Street with very few vehicles. Beyond the clock tower are the Melton Mowbray road and the route out to Loughborough. Changes have radically altered the scene in the last forty years.

Top left: Richard III, King of England, was killed on Bosworth Field in 1485 and his body was carried across the back of a horse to be buried in Leicester. Henry VIII requested that the body be excavated and Richard's remains cast into the river off Bow Bridge. *Above*: The Old Blue Boar Inn, Leicester, where Richard III spent his last night. This is a reproduction of a lithograph drawn on stone by John Flower.

West Bridge, Leicester, by John Flower: a lithograph drawn on stone. This is an illustration of the old bridge which crossed the River Soar in the eighteenth century. This and the lithograph top right were published in 1826.

Left: The River Soar, Leicester, *c.* 1920. The remains of the castle mound run down to the river. *Above*: Leicester Castle, 1791, drawing by J. Throsby, engraved by J. Walker. This image shows the River Soar and the remains of Leicester Castle, which was built during the Norman conquest in the eleventh century.

Bandstand in Victoria Park, 1923. Leicestershire soldiers who returned from the First World War play nostalgic tunes.

Above: A remarkable view of the entrance to the regimental barracks, off the Newarke, Leicester, before the First World War. *Right*: Gateway in the 'Neworks', drawn on stone by John Flower, 1826.

Leicester Abbey, *c*. 1790. It was damaged during the occupation by the Royalists in the Civil War of the seventeenth century.

The abbey ruins, 1912.

Clock tower, 1907. This postcard illustrates well the local traders, who served the community.

Granby Street, 1904. This road had developed into one of the major stagecoach routes out of Leicester during the late eighteenth century. The Three Crowns, a famous hostelry, was a most important centre for delivery of mail and parcels. (Refer to the photograph reproduced at the top of page 100.) After the demise of the coach trade this hostelry was converted into the National Provincial Bank.

Midland station, London Road, 1904. It opened on 5 May 1840.

The Old Pack Horse Inn, 246 Belgrave Gate, *c.* 1900. The following were landlords: John Gibbins 1862–3; William Lowe 1877–91; Richard Pick 1900. In 1846 it was 222 Belgrave Gate. In 1835 it was just Belgrave Gate, with no reference to the Pack Horse business.

West Bridge, 1914.

Captured German guns displayed in Leicester, close to the museum, December 1918.

Freeman, Hardy & Willis, Humberstone Gate, 1940s. This area is detailed on the German map below.

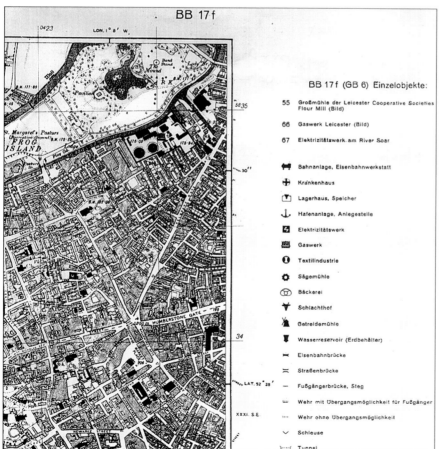

BB 17f

BB 17f (GB 6) Einzelobjekte:

55 Großmühle der Leicester Cooperative Societies Flour Mill (Bild)

66 Gaswerk Leicester (Bild)

67 Elektrizitätswerk am River Soar

🚂 Bahnanlage, Eisenbahnwerkstatt

✚ Krankenhaus

▼ Lagerhaus, Speicher

⚓ Hafenanlage, Anlegestelle

🔋 Elektrizitätswerk

🏭 Gaswerk

❶ Textilindustrie

⚙ Sägemühle

⊕ Bäckerei

🐂 Schlachthof

🌀 Getreidemühle

▮ Wasserreservoir (Erdbehälter)

⊢⊣ Eisenbahnbrücke

⊨ Straßenbrücke

— Fußgängerbrücke, Steg

⊔ Wehr mit Übergangsmöglichkeit für Fußgänger

···· Wehr ohne Übergangsmöglichkeit

⌄ Schleuse

)⊂⊃(Tunnel

'Leicester Militargeer Angabon nach den bir zum 15:01:1942 vorhandenen Unterlagen.' Humberstone Gate is shown on the map, which was 'captured' by Bernard Fawkes of Wymondham on a German airfield somewhere in Belgium in 1945.

99

Left: Coach leaving the Three Crowns Hotel on Granby Street, *c.* 1860.

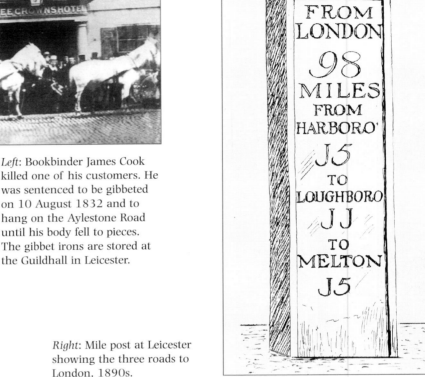

Left: Bookbinder James Cook killed one of his customers. He was sentenced to be gibbeted on 10 August 1832 and to hang on the Aylestone Road until his body fell to pieces. The gibbet irons are stored at the Guildhall in Leicester.

Right: Mile post at Leicester showing the three roads to London, 1890s.

Right: A block cut by Rigby Graham for a broadsheet *Execution of a Bookbinder, James Cook* (1966).

Much has been written about the achievements of Leicestershire County Cricket Club, Leicester Rugby Club and Leicester City Football Club. The next two pages cover only a few of their sporting triumphs. So much more could be said than space allows.

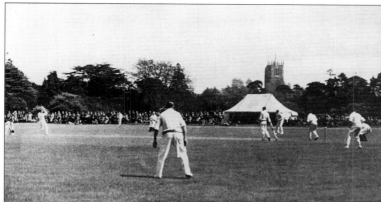

Top left: Leicestershire and Nottinghamshire Cricket Club at Aylestone Road, 1939.
Top right: W.G. Grace (with beard) watching the action during his last match at Leicester, 1904. He was playing for London County. *Left*: Leicestershire *v* Somerset at Egerton Park, Melton Mowbray, 1949.

This sculpture commemorates the county's three famous sporting clubs. All three were cup winners in the mid-1990s. This splendid record was erected through *Leicester Mercury* sponsorship. The bronze statue was designed by Martin Williams and marks the achievements of Leicester City FC (Coca Cola Cup winners, 1996/7), Leicester Tigers Rugby Club (Pilkington Cup winners, 1996/7), Leicestershire County·Cricket Club (Britannic Assurance County Champions, 1996 and 1998). It stands at the entrance to Humberstone Gate in the centre of Leicester.

Arthur Chandler and George Richie of Leicester City putting pressure on the Sunderland goalkeeper, 17 November 1928. Arthur scored the winning goal in the 1–0 victory at Filbert Street.

The Worthington Cup final at Wembley, Saturday 21 March 1999. Leicester City came second to Tottenham Hotspur. In this photograph the excited City fans are walking through to Wembley. Young supporter Amy Grech, with her Leicester City blue nose provided by the *Leicester Mercury* and hat, waits to go into the ground.

The Worthington Cup final. Leicester City and Tottenham Hotspur walk out on to the ground. It was a memorable occasion, but unfortunately there had to be a winner on the famous Wembley turf. Nielsen scored the winning goal for Tottenham at 90 minutes!

Blaby

Kirby Muxloe Castle. The brick-built structure was produced to a design recommended by Lord Hastings of Ashby Castle and work began in about 1480. Lord Hastings was beheaded in June 1483 on the orders of Richard III, and Shakespeare records Hastings' demise:

> O bloody Richard! Miserable England,
> I prophecy the fearfullest time to thee.
> That ever wretched age hath looked upon.
> Miserable England – what times.

In fact it was wonderful England – the village rose again! War damage hit the area around Kirby Muxloe again during 1941. Houses that were bombed were eventually repaired, and have blended back into the village scene. The ruined castle remains.

KIRBY MUXLOE

The brick-covered Kirby Muxloe Castle inside its moat. It was built at a time when design ideas had moved on to include stronger defensive measures, and was impossible to defend against specialised cannon.

On 28 January 1941 the *Leicester Chronicle* stated that Kirby Muxloe was the most bomb-battered village in Britain. William Forrest wrote that this village stood up to a blitz and 'every wrecked home is being restored'. Not one life was lost but the Free Church was demolished.

GLENFIELD

Kirby Road. This image and the two photographs below were taken in Glenfield before the First World War.

Park Gate (*left*) and The Round Hill (*below*).

THURLASTON

Thurlaston bellringers, Christmas 1906.

The popular cartoon featuring Weary Willie and Tired Tim was published in a variety of newspapers before the First World War. *Above*: a drawing of Weary Willie, after Bert Thomas, *c.* 1914. *Left*: an interpretation of the characters by Thurlaston villagers at a village fête, just before the First World War.

ENDERBY

Cross Street, with the Dog and Gun Inn, before the First
World War. The brewer was Joseph Frost.

The remains of Enderby Quarry, a line drawing by Rigby
Graham, 23 November 1981.

Packhorse bridge, 1993. This is undoubtedly the most
interesting of all the packhorse bridges that have survived
in this part of the Midlands. The two-arched structure was
built in the fertile water meadows south of the village of
Enderby. Numerous fords once existed over the many
streams located between Enderby and Whetstone but
because the land was low lying an extensive causeway was
built to convey traffic along in time of flood. As a result
there was a need for a packhorse bridge. It originally
crossed one of the tributaries feeding the River Soar that
rise in the Narborough Bog but over the last 200 years
extensive drainage has taken place in this area, altering
the line of the ancient water-courses. Today numerous
large boulders weighing up to 3 tons still lie along the
edge of a drainage ditch that forms the headland and the
causeway leading to the stone bridge. These heavy stones
were uncovered over the centuries during ploughing
operations in the fields to the south of the village of Enderby. They were then moved and positioned in a line as a flood
protection barrier. A water-mill stood on this site in 1086 and may have been built by Ulf, the Saxon overlord who farmed
the meadows in this area at the time of the Domesday survey. Mills continued to be operated on this site continuously for
over 900 years. The last one finally ceased grinding corn in 1957.

NARBOROUGH

The road through Narborough, 1920s. This is now the A46.

Narborough railway station in 1904 when Sidney Jones was Stationmaster. The station opened on 1 January 1864 and closed on 4 March 1968.

The Rectory, in 1904, home of the Revd Thomas Barker Hardy MA.

BLABY

The Red Cow Inn, 1920s.

Entrance to Blaby via Countesthorpe Road, 1920s.

Blaby Mill, 1880s. The mill was owned by the Vice family. Bladi (Blaby) is mentioned in the Domesday survey as having a mill, possibly on the same site by a tributary of the River Soar. It is well hidden off the track past Blaby cemetery.

COSBY

Above: St Michael and All Angels' church and the bridge, 1928. The Vicar at the time was the Revd Gilbert Augustus James BA.

Right: The mill, Cosby Road, out towards Broughton Astley, pre-1907. This mill was also owned by the Vice family of Blaby.

Cosby village before the First World War. The bridges were protected by railings, so the shallow stream was obviously subject to repeated flooding.

CROFT

Croft House, rectory and the church of
St Michael in a beautiful setting by the River
Soar, *c.* 1925. The Vicar was the Revd John
Casson MA.

Croft Hill. This verse was written by an anonymous
Leicester gentlemen in 1821. In those days this was
treeless hill!

Behold Croft Hill with stately pride arise;
Ambitious, it aspires to reach the skies,
No humble shrubs, no lofty trees there grow
To shade its beauty from the vale below.
The fleecy flocks here browse with sweet delight,
And crop the flowers upon its topmost height;
The sides an everlasting verdure wear,
Which, smiling, say 'tis summer all the year,
See Thurlaston's brook below meandering glides,
And slowly creep along its narrow sides;
The fishes here, forgetful of their state,
Now sport and play, then glide to certain fate.

The London & North Western Down goods
train passing through Croft station with a
0–6–0 4F designed by Fowler, 1911. The
station opened on 1 January 1864 and closed
on 4 March 1968.

STONEY STANTON

The parish church of St Michael, *c.* 1916. The Vicar was the Revd Anthony Edward Denny Disney, who was appointed in 1885.

These two photographs record the unveiling of the memorial cross to the fallen of the First World War, 17 January 1921. It bears an all too long list of the names of the village men who did not return from the battlefields.

Bosworth

Market Bosworth, 1982. The very small market town is about 3 miles north of the site of the famous Battle of Bosworth, which witnessed the death of one King and the crowning of another. Here Richard III was killed and Henry VII became the first monarch of the Tudor dynasty. His successors included Henry VIII and Elizabeth I, the great Tudor queen, who defeated the Spanish Armada. A weekly market has been held here since 1285 and cattle are sold in auctions next to a nearby public house. This is where local people traditionally traded their cheeses, cattle, eggs and many other types of produce.

BURBAGE

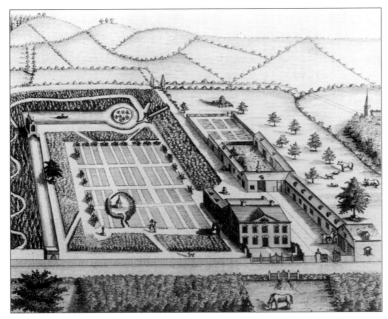

The Manor House, the home of David Wells at Burbage (Burbach), 1810. Note the formal gardens, stables and dovecote.

The Old Grange, a splendid half-timbered cottage, 1917.

Horsepool House, 1913. On the right two ladies and a bowler-hatted gentleman are looking over the iron gate and railings.

HINCKLEY

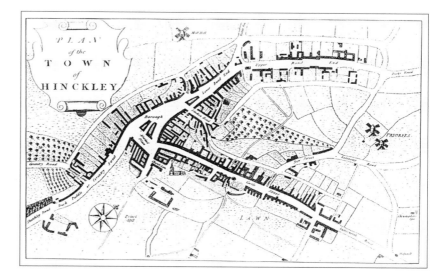

The town of Hinckley by J. Robinson, 1782. Clearly indicated are Sketchley Road, Duck Paddle or Coventry Road, Market Place, Borough, Lower Band End, Upper Road End, Derby Road, New Street, Leicester Road. Three mills – two at the Priories and one at Mill Hill – are shown.

Features on the plan shown above are the Borough and the Market Place. This picture shows the area in about 1905 with the distinctive street lamp. The Town Hall Arms is behind the lamp; W. Bonnett was in charge of the premises.

The Borough, 1922. The Union Hotel is in the centre of the photograph; it was owned by Ernest S. Randle.

Leicester Road, looking out towards the Priories, *c.* 1920.

E. Allsop Ltd in the centre of Hinckley on what is now the A47, *c.* 1920.

A group of lads walking to school down London Road, 1920s.

Priesthill Road, 1920s.

Left: Mount Hill Road, 1920s.

Hollycroft Hill, 1920s.

Hinckley Windmill standing to the north of the town, *c.* 1890. In the late nineteenth century it was worked by William Cooper but was demolished in the 1890s.

EARL SHILTON

A view of Lower Hinckley Road, 1920s.

Earl Shilton Union Mill, 1911. It was built in 1800 as a tower-mill by a group of forty-one shareholders. They rented out the mill to a variety of millers who worked it until well into the First World War. It was struck by lightning in 1917, then stood as a ruin and was finally demolished in the 1940s.

Station Street, 1920s.

KIRBY MALLORY

Dark Lane, before the First World War. Kirby Mallory is a delightful little village close to Mallory Park where considerable changes have since taken place since the beginning of the twentieth century.

Incredible classic motor vehicles race around the course at Mallory Park, 1998. On the left is John Baker-Courtenay driving his Westfield SE.

These three views are all from the 1998 season at Mallory Park. Here spectators sit on the raised bank in front of the starting line to get a good view of the beginning of a race. The Sunbeam 'Tigress' is the car closest to the spectators.

The famous Sunbeam 'Tigress' before the classic race. John Baker-Courtenay is sitting in the machine. The late Bob Roberts spent ten years rebuilding the machine. Sunbeam designer Louis Coatalen designed two cars in 1925 – 'Tiger' and 'Tigress'. Major Henry O.D. Segrave achieved a new world land speed record in the 'Tiger' on the sands at Southport, Lancashire, in 1926.

The 'Tigress' world land speed record car rounding a bend in the lead, driven by John Baker-Courtenay. He dedicated the race to the memory of driver Bob Gerard.

DESFORD

High Street, August 1911.

Church Lane, July 1906.

Desford water-mill, *c.* 1970. A mill was first mentioned on this site in 1140. Water was drawn from the Bagworth Brook. The mill ceased operating in the 1920s.

Desford airfield, 1940. This hangar was erected on the north-west side of Peckleton Lane and just emerging from it is a Boulton & Paul Defiant. At this stage it was an RAF secret weapon, but unfortunately the Luftwaffe found many weaknesses in the design.

A Vickers Armstrong Wellington standing at the side of the hangar off Peckleton Lane, early 1940. This was a visitor from 38 Squadron based at RAF Marham in Norfolk. It would have been unusual to see such a plane at Desford as this was an elementary training field.

The airfield no longer exists. The site off Peckleton Lane is now part of Caterpillar Tractors. This is now the view of the area seen in the two photographs above.

RATBY

Leicestershire County Cricket Club second
team at T. Jayes' benefit match, 27 May 1912.

The school, 1925. Walter Baker was the
master and Miss M.E. Ramsey was the
infants' mistress.

Ratby post-mill, 1902. The exact site of the mill is now
difficult to located, although remains were found near Ratby
just before the First World War. In the 1891 A.T. Cufflin is
listed as miller at Ratby.

GROBY

The Old Hall, *c.*1910.

These two unusual photographs were taken on 14 August 1909. They record the erection of a cattle trough by Groby parish on the day it was brought into use by Muriel Everard, with her husband Thomas Everard JP and director of Everard's Brewery – 'A merciful man is merciful to his beast.' The trough was financed by the Drinking Fountain & Cattle Trough Association, 70 Victoria Street, London. A granite trough provided water for passing cattle and the working horses, which only reigned on the land for a few more years. The car, traction and steam-engines were soon to supersede horse-drawn vehicles and ploughs. The main works of the Patent Victoria Stone Company, which made the trough, produced fashioned granite that was used for flagging in cities throughout Great Britain.

NEWBOLD VERDON

Main Street, early 1940s.

Church Row, *c.* 1914.

The Jubilee Inn, a beer house on Main
Street, before the First World War.

MARKET BOSWORTH

Bosworth Hall, 1791, drawn by J. Throsby and engraved by J. Walker. The hall on the right has changed little since the last eighteenth century (see below). On the left stands the church of St Peter.

A photograph taken during the 1980s after the hall had been converted into a hospital. Now it is a luxury hotel.

Market Place, *c.* 1905.

Sutton Lane, *c.* 1920.

Park Street, *c,* 1920.

A photograph published in about 1905 detailing King Dick's well. This stone cairn was built over the actual well in 1813 by the antiquary Samuel Parr. The site is between Sutton Cheney and Shenton, south of Market Bosworth, and it is believed that Richard III drank from this well in 1485.

Two stone monuments, 1982. They mark the graves of horses buried in the park by the squire from the hall, Charles Tollemache Scott. The plaques on the monuments record the names of three fine chargers, the last of which was interred here in 1892.

BARWELL

High Street, 1916. On the left stands the Queen's Head public house. Its landlord was William Powers.

Shilton Road, 1916.

Mill Street, photographed by G. Farman, 1920s. The brew house in the background sold Aucott's Ales and Guinness stout.

TWYCROSS

The gibbet near Twycross, 1984. The murderer John Massey was hanged and his remains were then exhibited on this gibbet in February 1800. Massey killed his wife by kicking her into the mill stream. He was hanged at Red Hill, Birstall. His body – soon a skeleton – was suspended on this gibbet for twenty years as a warning to others!

Founding a zoo began as only an idea for Molly Badham and Nathalie Evans in 1954. But in 1963 they started the zoo at Twycross. Chimpanzees opened the premises! Considerable changes have taken place since then and now Twycross is a conservation and education centre. A fine breeding programme concentrates on many rare and threatened animals.

Above: The Asian elephants at the zoo are part of a very successful breeding programme. *Right*: Bonobo chimpanzees are a close relation of the human species. They enjoy their life at Twycross and are raising a family, part of a programme to combat the threat of their extinction.

SHEEPY PARVA

Sheepy Mill, 1910. The fine, imposing water-mill stood prominently on the Sheepy Magna to Sheepy Parva road.

Power for the mill was provided by water from the River Sence via a breast-shot wheel of about 14 feet in diameter. It operated throughout the nineteenth century. This drawing illustrates the mechanism.

Sheepy Mill photographed from the river, 1974. At this time it was due for demolition and had long since ceased to grind corn using the traditional method. A water-mill was listed on this site in the eleventh-century Domesday records.

North-West

Weighbridge Office Colearton   Newbold 89

The weighbridge office, Colearton, near Newbold, 1989. Between 1975 and 1980 the artist Rigby Graham travelled around Leicestershire recording the mines, quarries, properties threatened with demolition, disused railway lines and bridges. He noted the changes that were taking place and were destroying the Victorian structures of the county. Ten years after Rigby finished his tour there are no coal mines in Leicestershire, and almost all their buildings have been demolished.

In 1976 a new development was begun – the building of the large reservoir in Rutland. Originally called Empingham reservoir (now Rutland Water) it is an amazing example of twentieth-century civil engineering and shows forward thinking for the benefit of generations to come. Yet the mining buildings that stood in these counties have almost all gone along with many quarries. The modern policy is to fill up part of the area with household waste – what a useless idea! Very few products actually need to be buried and most can now be recycled.

There is an odd survivor of the industry that once thrived here. At Swithland Wood, where mines were dug during the nineteenth century, some buildings have been preserved and this is now a site of special scientific interest because of the wildlife that exists in the surrounding countryside.

Fortunately, Rigby was aware of the threat from the future and he was determined to record the legacy of the past, through allowing his illustrations to be published in many books. His most important volume was *Leicestershire*.

CASTLE DONINGTON

Donington Hall, drawing by W. Wilkins, engraved by J. Basire, 1792. Built in the style called Strawberry Hill Gothic at the end of the eighteenth century, today it is the headquarters of British Midland Airways.

Donington Hall with the deer running in the park, c. 1917. The site was a prisoner-of war camp for German officers at this time. The huts surrounded by wire housed the British guards.

The Cedar, High Street, home of
Thomas S. Starkie, 1925.

The Old Key House, *c.* 1925. The house
was built in 1574. A vagrant hanged
himself on the key in the lock on the
front door, in the sixteenth century.

The Barroon, a convalescent home for
Nottingham women, 1916. Miss
Martha Millington, the matron, is
standing at the doorway.

135

Ferry crossing the Trent at Kings Mills, near Castle Donington, *c*. 1906.

Castle Donington tower-mill, 1910. The small three-storey mill was built in 1773 by T. Wells. It operated until 1932 and was demolished in 1941. The site was then surveyed and converted into an airfield which opened in 1943 under the control of Bomber Command.

Left: The footpath leading to the village through Windmill Fields, 1904. In the background stands the church of St Luke. The Vicar was the Revd James Cusack Roney-Dougal BA.

East Midlands Airport, 1999. In January 1943 an airfield opened near Castle Donington as a wartime Bomber Command satellite to nearby RAF Wymeswold. In September 1946 the RAF airfield closed and was neglected for some time. However, the building of the nearby M1 motorway changed the situation drastically and made this an ideal site in the centre of England for a new airport, which opened in 1964. Here we can see the recently built departure lounge, overlooked by the air traffic control tower.

A British Midland aircraft standing on the apron at East Midlands Airport.

Holidaymakers boarding a Saab 340 departing from East Midlands Airport for Guernsey, July 1997.

The Donington Park race circuit is a magnificent site for Grand Prix racing for cars and motorcycles. Much of the development has evolved from the ideas of one man – Tom Wheatcroft – and today it is the home of the Donington Grand Prix Collection. Tom Wheatcroft, founder and owner of the Donington Grand Prix Collection, is pictured here with Tazio Nuvolari's 1934 Maserati 8CM and the 1936 Alfa Romeo Bimotore, both permanent exhibits from the collection.

The McLaren Hall, showing part of the Donington Grand Prix Collection.

BREEDON-ON-THE-HILL

The Roundhouse lock-up for criminals near the Hastings Arms public house, 1904. The landlord at this time was Joseph Liddington.

A delightful photograph of the stone bridge at The Green, *c.* 1910.

A drawing of Breedon quarry by Rigby Graham, 15 November 1981. Above the quarry cliffs the tower of the church of St Mary and Hardulph is just visible.

COALVILLE

A photograph published in about 1905 of the old oak tree that once stood on the corner of Donington Road, Coalville. It was then estimated to have been standing for two centuries.

Mrs Wallis on Donington Road, 1910.

Station Road, 1904. On the left stands the shop of Benjamin Bishop Drewett, draper.

Belvoir Road and the Wesleyan chapel, 1905. On the right stands Lindleys House.

Belvoir Road with Lloyds Bank on the left, 1920s.

London Road, 1904.

High Street, 1904. On the right are the premises of James Gutteridge, boot dealer and grocer, next door to William Hill, junior, who promised the 'best value' for groceries and provisions.

Aerial view of Coalville, *c.* 1920.

The level-crossing with a steam train crossing the highway, holding up the traffic in front of the Coalville Savings Bank on what is now the A50, 1920s.

WHITWICK AND MOUNT ST BERNARD ABBEY

Thatched cottages around the Market Place, 1903.

'Pride of the Forest' bus standing in the Market Place, 1925. It conveyed passengers between Shepshed, Whitwick and Coalville. Just to the left of the bus is the post office; Mrs Nellie Harris was the post mistress.

A view of Cademan Street from Castle Hill, c. 1925.

Pare's Hill, 1904. In the centre is the Crown and Cushion, offering fine ales, and to the right is the Railway Hotel – Mrs Jane May was the proprietor.

Silver Street, *c.* 1910.

The reading cloister at Mount St Bernard Abbey, Whitwick. The modern Cistercian abbey was founded in 1835 by Ambrose Phillips de Lisle Esq., of Grace Dieu, and was raised to the status of a mitred abbey in 1848. Father Bernard was the first abbot. This was the first Catholic abbey built and then used continuously in England since the Reformation. Pugin designed it.

The refectory, Mount St Bernard Abbey, *c.* 1910.

The monks raising crops in their garden, *c.* 1905.

A monk mining granite in a local quarry, *c.* 1910. The
stone was used in walls and for buildings.

SNARESTONE

Thatched cottages on the main street, *c.* 1925.

A fine line of thatched cottages standing along Church Lane, *c.* 1920.

IBSTOCK

The church of St Denys, viewed from the west, an illustration by Mr Malcolm, 1795.

The church of St Denys, 1904. The Vicar was the Revd Samuel Flood MA.

Ibstock war memorial was erected to the memory of the men of the parish who fell in the First World War.

MEASHAM

Ashby Road, *c.* 1915.

'Big Basin' on the Ashby-de-la-Zouch canal. Work to open the canal up so that it could carry coal from the Measham wharfs began on 19 April 1804. A poor return on the investment was reported by Joseph Wilkes of Measham.

MOIRA

Station Road,
c. 1925.

The Moira Pottery Company stoneware
manufacturers off the Crescent. *c.* 1920.

Ashby canal, *c.* 1910. Barges are
moving down the cut and there
are passers-by on the tow-path.

STAUNTON HAROLD

The Earl Ferrers, a peer of the realm who lived at Staunton Hall, died on the scaffold at Tyburn (now the site of Marble Arch) on 21 April 1760. Ferrers shot his steward with his pistol solely as a result of his violent temper. He received short shrift when he appeared for trial before his colleagues in the House of Lords. He hanged for one hour, was then disembowelled and his remains were put on public display for five days. This engraving by W. Walker is from a drawing by John Throsby showing the hall and grounds in 1789, twenty-nine years after Ferrers' death.

In 1904 this was the home of the Right Honourable Earl Ferrers MA, DL, JP. Earl Ferrers' descendants seem to have suffered little as a result of his actions but how did the descendants of steward John Johnson fare? Visit Breedon-on-the-Hill and read the inscription upon the gravestone in the churchyard.

Staunton Harold, 1985. It was purchased by Leonard Cheshire VC as a home for the terminally ill.

DONINGTON-LE-HEATH

Manor House Farm, early 1980s. The old first-floor entrances are clearly visible. This is now a museum.

Richard III slept in this bed in the White Boar, one of the most important inns in Leicester, during the night of 20/21 August 1485. King Richard did not sleep well because 'there appeared about him diverse fearful ghosts, running about him suffering him to take any rest, still crying revenge'. Two days later he was killed on Redmoor Plain during the Battle of Bosworth. The landlord immediately changed the name of the establishment to the Blue Boar Inn. The old inn was demolished in 1838. This vast bed remained empty for obvious reasons and passed from tenant to the tenant. In about 1580 the bedstead collapsed and a secret drawer was disclosed; it held gold coins left by the dead King to the value of £300. The landlord Thomas Clarke, suddenly a very wealthy man, became Mayor of Leicester in 1583. The bedstead was rebuilt for his use. Remarkably this famous bedstead, which has been altered over the years, still survives and is now displayed at the Manor House, Donington-le-Heath. This engraving was produced for publication in about 1790.

151

ASHBY-DE-LA-ZOUCH

Ashby-de-la-Zouch Castle with the church of St Helen to the right, drawing by John Throsby engraved by J. Walker, 1790. During the Civil War in the winter of 1642/3, the Royalist commander in the Midlands, Henry Hastings, used the castle as his headquarters and set up garrisons at Swarkeston, Kings Mills, Wilne Ferry and Belvoir Castle. However, his forces were no match for the dedicated soldiers of Cromwell. On 4 March 1646, with his troops blighted by disease, Henry surrendered the castle.

Ashby Castle was destroyed by the Parliamentarians' cannon. This photograph was taken in 1982.

Ashby Castle, an aerial view, 1982.

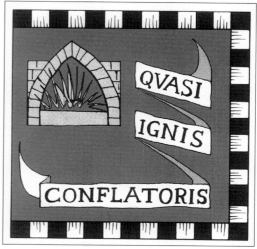

The coat-of-arms of Colonel-General Henry Hastings (Lord Loughborough).

Left: The King's flag hung from this tower during the Civil War. This photograph was taken in 1982.

Ashby-de-la-Zouch, viewed from above the castle, 1925.

A Burton and Ashby light railway tram in front of the Royal Hotel on Station Road, *c.* 1910.

A crowd singing a hymn on Market Street to mark the coronation of King George V. He became King in 1910 and was crowned in 1911. Grocer W.A. Haynes from 12 Market Street is at the front of the photograph in a trilby hat.

William Morley Hatton's grocery shop, 51 Market Street, 1925.

Light railway tram on Burton Road, 27 August 1915.

Ashby-de-la-Zouch post-mill being used as a chicken coop, 1917. It was built in 1835 and ceased working in about 1900. The last man to run it was a Mr Jarvis. It was pulled down in 1920.

Rawden Terrace and Bath Street with the light railway tram, *c.* 1905.

Remains of the light railway track near the station approach, 1990s.

Market Street, 1904. William Alfred Haynes, grocer, was at 7 Market Street, John Holdron, ironmonger and agricultural implement dealer, in Market Street and Mrs Anne Tyler, ladies' outfitter, was at 16 Market Street.

Market Street, *c.* 1910.

The Bull's Head, 1925. It is now the Fayre and Firkin and has undergone only a few exterior changes.

RAVENSTONE WITH SNIBSTON

On 29 September 1894 the two villages became the civil parish of Ravenstone with Snibston. This photograph shows Ravenstone village in 1910. In the background stands the church of St Michael with its very low spire. The Vicar was the Revd Alfred Sydney Dowling AK, CL.

Snibston Discovery Park, 1999. In the background stands Snibston colliery, a feature of the past that has been preserved for the future. All the underground coal mines in Leicestershire have now closed but this site is a spectacular record of this once important industry.

'Science for industry', a remarkable display at Snibston. The exhibition hall is one of the leading science attractions for youngsters and the young at heart in Great Britain. This photograph shows a beam engine which still works today. Originally it drew water from a local reservoir.

Bibliography

Ashton, N., *Leicestershire Water-mills*, 1977

Bailey , B.J., *Portrait of Leicestershire*, 1977

Burton, D.R., *Loughborough in Old Photographs*, 1997

Butt, R.V.J., *Railway Stations*, 1995

Canter, L. *The Historic Country Houses of Leicestershire and Rutland*, 1998

Clayton, M., *Foxhunting in Paradise*, 1993

Crocker, J., (ed.) *Charnwood Forest and Changing Landscape*, 1981

Graham, R., *Leicestershire*, 1980

Hager's Directory, *County of Leicester*, 1849

Halpenny, B.B., *Action Stations 2*, 1981

Hill, J.H., *The History of Market Harborough*, 1875

Hoskins, W.G., *A Shell Guide: Leicestershire*, 1970

Kelly's Directory, *Leicestershire and Rutland, 1900, 1904, 1916, 1925, 1941*

Moon, N., *Leicestershire and Rutland Windmills*, 1981

Nichols, J., *History and Antiquities of the County of Leicester*, 4 vols, 1795–1815

Old English Towns and Hotels, 1999

Palmer, R., *The Folklore of Leicestershire and Rutland*, 1985

Pevsner, N., *Leicestershire and Rutland*, 1984

Stevens, P.A. *The Leicester and Melton Mowbray Navigations*, 1992

Stevenson, J., *A Family Guide to Bradgate Park and Swithland Wood*, 1979

Tew, D., *Throsby Revisited*, 1989

Webb, E.A.H., *The 17th Regiment*, 1912

Webster, V. Raymond, *Medieval Timber Framed Houses in Leicestershire*, 1983

White, W. (ed.), *Leicestershire and Rutland*, 1846

Wylly, H.C., *The Leicestershire Regiment*, 1928

The church of St Mary's at Breedon-on-the-Hill, April 1976, watercolour illustration by Rigby Graham drawn for his book *Leicestershire*, possibly the finest production of its type ever released in the county. This magnificent book, a record for the future, has not yet been sufficiently recognised by the collectors of fine recorded history of our county.

Acknowledgements

Presenting memories as a collection in a book is an idea that has been in the back of the author's mind for many years. On a suggestion from Sutton Publishing it became a fact during the winter of 1998, and the author was able to bring together photographs that had been acquired from a number of people over many decades but that had lain dormant. Help from friends extended the collection. The author's grateful thanks are extended to: Rosemary and Keith Badcock; Edwina Baker-Courtenay, Brooksby Hall; John Baker-Courtenay; Clare Brandish, Ragdale Hall; Kathryn Brown, Tumbledown Farm; Beattie Cross; Chris Foster, Long Clawson Dairy; Rigby Graham; Mrs V.J. Richards, Twycross Zoo; Nick Rooney; V. Raymond Webster; Edgar Wilford; Tom Wheatcroft, Donington Park. Thanks are due to Pat Peters for processing the manuscript for the publisher's use. The majority of the images are out of copyright or the photograph belongs to the author. Where copyright has been retained, permission has been granted to publish. Should the author be unaware of the infringement of copyright, he offers his sincere apologies and will make an immediate apology.

These photographs date from 1930. The first was taken off Swan Nest in the River Eye at Saxby Road, Melton Mowbray, and the second shows children diving into the mill pond below the sluice at the site of Abbot's water-mill, Garthorpe. They recall long-forgotten golden memories of activities before the Second World War that are an impossibility today.

Selective Index